TYPICAL ENGLISH VILLAGES

WHAT SHALL WE DO WITH OUR BOYS

HOVSES FOR PEOPLE WITH HOB~BIES

Window-pane Rhymes.

SPORT IN OTHER LANDS
BIG GAME IN INDIA.

LITERARY NOTES

AT · THE · THEATRE

FLOWER & FRUIT FARMS OF GREAT BRITAIN
Vegetables And . . . . Flowers . . From Seed.

THE . . . STEAM POACHER.

COUNTRY LIFE

1897~1997

THE

ENGLISH ARCADIA

COUNTRY LIFE
1897~1997
THE
ENGLISH
ARCADIA
ROY STRONG

COUNTRY LIFE BOOKS
and
BOXTREE

Produced by Country Life Books, Kings Reach Tower, Stamford Street, London SE1 9LS
First published in Great Britain in 1996
by Boxtree Limited, Broadwall House, 21 Broadwall, London SE1 9PL

Publisher: Juliet Matthews
Editor: Mark Irving
Design: RUBIK Graphic Communications
Production: Roger Bonnett

CONTENTS

Preface

The task of writing this book would have been impossible without the enthusiasm and open-mindedness of Clive Aslet, the present editor of *Country Life*. I am very grateful to Mr Michael Tree for filling the gap in my own collection of the magazine by loaning the volumes from 1897 to the 1950s which belonged to his remarkable mother, Mrs Nancy Lancaster. Three other sets were also utilised: one in the London Library, another in the archive of my old stomping ground of the National Portrait Gallery, and the set belonging to *Country Life's* photographic archive.

The moment to write a history of *Country Life* is apposite, for in the last fifteen years there has been a flood of revisionist books on the history of the countryside. My debt to their refreshing, if occasionally iconoclastic, attitudes will be apparent in the text. Although this is not a history of the internal machinations of the magazine, I have benefited from some enlightening conversations with former members of the magazine's staff. Camilla Costello, the librarian of the magazine's archive, put up with the incursion of both the book's editor and myself and guided us through the mountain of visual material which is one of the magazine's glories. The publisher at IPC, Juliet Matthews, has shown an unflagging and sophisticated interest in the book's progress, and the copy-editing skills of Rachel Rogers and Rachel Pearce have been invaluable. A great debt is owed to Dawn Ryddner, whose design for the book called for a keen understanding of the juxtaposition of word and image.

Mark Irving has been my tolerant editor as I have laboured through the decades of volumes, and the resulting text and placement of images owes a great deal to his pertinent criticisms and perception.

Country Life is an institution commonly thought of as merely illustrating a comforting vision of an upper class never-never-land. In fact, its history is very different and impinges on ideas and images which have been central to this country's national consciousness during the past century. For a magazine to have attained such an iconic status is rare, and reflects profoundly on its impact over this period and sets a standard to be followed if the magazine is to flourish for a second century.

ROY STRONG, January 1996

The New Bored.
'All move up one higher,' said he, with a wave of his hand.

Introduction

My earliest memories of *Country Life* date from the late 1950s, when I was an assistant keeper at the National Portrait Gallery. Each day at about 4.30 pm, the senior staff gathered in the director's office, which was also the boardroom, for tea. A warder placed a tray ready for one of us to brew up and each person poured a cup and sat down at the vast table which took up most of the room. Words were few, the silence being broken only by occasional questions such as "How many Duchesses of Bedford are there at the moment?" or "Do you know of anyone who's got into Barrington Court?" Otherwise, heads were bowed low over the magazines which were laid out at one end of the room. The lucky early bird always made off with *Country Life*.

The magazine allowed me a glimpse of a world into which I had not been born. I had started life in a 1920s terrace house in North London, and my earliest glimpse of a great country house was Hatfield, in about 1950, which I had reached by a Green Line bus. I was fascinated by it and by all things old and English. This was hardly surprising, for my childhood had been spent in a war throughout which an overt patriotism had been expressed by the romantic images immortalised in *Country Life*, revealing a cast of village, manor house and rolling landscape, cathedral, castle and historic city. It would never have occurred to me to question its conception of this country's national identity, one which was so utterly different from my own suburban upbringing. Indeed, two of my earliest books, given as school prizes, were Batsford ones on English castles and cathedrals, which I had chosen myself. But as I turned the pages of *Country Life*, I peered into a world of which I was to become part, one occupied by old houses, historic artifacts, and concerned with conservation, restoration issues and what was later to become termed "the heritage experience".

The National Portrait Gallery has always been connected with the great houses and their vast picture collections. When I was there, their owners would occasionally drop in like visiting dignitaries to be received with due

(Opposite Title page) England as Arcady. The Chapel at Gibside, Northumberland.

(Opposite Preface) Olde England re-created. The Garden at Plas Brondanw, Gwynedd.

(Previous page) The eternal vision. Chiswick House and gardens, London, in 1897.

(Opposite) The cover of a mock edition of the magazine put together by the staff, showing the magazine's roots in earlier publications, such as the remarkable Country Life Books imprint.

Leaves from the Family Tree
in
COVENT GARDEN

Country Life Library

The Garden

Our Homes & Gardens

Country Life

Racing Illustrated

Navy & Army

Famous Cricketers

Famous Footballers

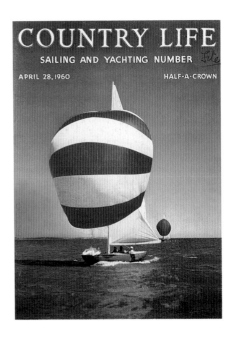

(Above) A cover from 1960.

deference by the director of the time. Within that world, *Country Life* occupied a unique status as a magazine for it was viewed as somehow not tarred with the squalid brush of journalism: its aura glowing with establishment values, assured and immutable.

By the 1960s, I was writing occasionally for the magazine, and a friendship blossomed with John Cornforth, one of its most distinguished architectural editors. He always referred to *Country Life* as if it were a physical entity, pronouncing which particular subject or attitude was or was not *Country Life*. In retrospect, the magazine's environment, even in 1960, was unashamedly elitist and rather old-fashioned. In visual terms it was anti-Modernist, and certainly anti any form of contemporary art, with the exception of John Piper and Lawrence Whistler; Henry Moore was never mentioned. The Royal Academy Summer Exhibition was reviewed but, apart from that, only exhibitions of old masters featured.

The magazine always had a compulsively romantic feel, no issue being without its "This England" cover. The other great draw was the article on a country house. Such houses always held an extraordinary fascination, for no one ever seemed to live in them. One's eye ran over the deserted rooms and garden vistas, all immaculate, and one was hypnotised by their beauty but also by that compelling void. What had happened to the owners? Didn't they have children and dogs? Did a copy of even *The Times* never enter the drawing room or a pair of slippers litter a bedroom floor? Somehow the superiority of their owners lay in the abdication of any visual presence.

This was always a magazine in which to go for a walk (even if at that date it was almost always in black and white) along passage ways, across halls and up staircases, through reception rooms and into bedrooms. But these were houses seemingly devoid of kitchens, sculleries, utility rooms or even bathrooms. These were gardens without tools and potting sheds, compost heaps or kitchen gardens.

But houses were not the only "unoccupied" features. So too were historic towns, villages and, for the most part, the landscape. There was nothing the photographer could do about parked cars, but otherwise the impression is given of a country which had been evacuated. The reader was the only human engaging with these vistas of ancient streets, sweeps of countryside or mellow villages. For some reason, all of this exerted a curious magic.

And then there was that girl on the frontispiece, always a head and shoulders, always smiling and always with a kind of aureole. The girls were rarely beautiful and the photographs were indifferent in quality, but who chose them and why were they presented as superior beings? In today's age of political correctness, they seem like sexist aberrations. But all of this ignores the magazine's greatest draw: the property pages. Their hold was total and as much time was spent dreaming about houses beyond one's income as in looking at the main contents.

In the 1970s, my relationship with the magazine became much closer. It was the decade where heritage concerns were first and foremost and *Country Life* had an unofficial alliance with the Victoria & Albert Museum, of which I was then director, in staging a series of polemical exhibitions between 1974 and 1979 on houses, churches and gardens. During this era, the magazine was the crucial — and successful — organ for the heritage lobby in its attempts to advance its cause.

By then, I had married and simultaneously "married" my wife's subscription to *Country Life*, copies of which were passed onto us by my father-in-law, Charles Oman. On his death we continued to take it and can now boast a complete run from about 1960, an invaluable resource if you have the space and can master the cryptic numbering system of the volumes. By the mid-1970s, we purchased a house in the country and, following many others before us, we turned to the magazine when it came to designing a large formal garden. I also reached for *Gardens Old and New*, those volumes published by *Country Life* which record the glorious pre-First World War era of country house garden design.

(Above) A cover from 1988.

After I resigned from the museum in 1987, the recently appointed editor of *Country Life*, Jenny Greene, asked me to contribute to what is now called 'Country Week'. I have been doing so ever since, and it is a source of great joy, for it involves writing about the ordinary things which make up the routine of late twentieth-century country living. I had no idea how many followed such activities until I met people who asked this or that about what I had written. When I was approached to write this book, I was initially enchanted by the idea of indulging in a wealth of nostalgia and friends said what fun I would have.

Having worked through about two thousand pages per year of up to a hundred volumes of *Country Life*, the fascinating story that was revealed was very different to what I had expected.

The present editor pointed out that there was really only one word to keep in my mind when writing the book — "country" — and this was advice to which I have adhered. But the word "country" embraces both an idea and a reality, and it is the interplay between these two occasionally opposing concepts which lies at the heart of this book.

Any magazine has both an internal and an external history. *Country Life's* internal history cannot be written as no archive exists, but if it had, it would have immeasurably complicated my task. It would not have altered my conclusions. Most people outside the magazine view it as having a single voice: this book is the story of how that voice arose and matured over a century.

ARCADIA
1897–1918

The Creators of Arcadia

By tradition *Country Life* was conceived on Walton Heath golf course in the Chilterns in about 1895. That seemingly trivial fact is deeply revealing. As a pastime, golf only moved south from Scotland during the 1890s and within twenty years some five hundred clubs were formed. The game developed at an apposite moment, for land was cheap due to the agricultural depression of the 1870s and was taken up with fervour by the sport-besotted late Victorian middle classes. Its competitiveness and individualism appealed to their professional and commercial instincts and extended into middle age the cult of public school athleticism familiar since childhood. Fresh-air scented discreet business conversations while the participants played out their roles as gentlemen amateurs, a status which called for both money and time, in a sport designed to exclude people devoid of what were regarded as the right social attributes. Golf consistently featured in the early decades of *Country Life* and it was to be its golfing correspondent, Bernard Darwin, who was to write the first history of the magazine. As we shall see, the occasion for its conception — a round of golf — was very apt: as a semi-rural sport played by members of the aspiring professional classes, it embraced both town and country.

The magazine's midwives were George, Lord Riddell and Edward Hudson and, probably, Sir George Newnes. The topic of conversation was "the production of a weekly illustrated paper of the highest quality that should get the best possible results from half-tone blocks". Hudson was by far the most important of the three but his companions tell us much about the magazine's conceptual hinterland. Sir George Newnes (1851-1910), the son of a Congregationalist minister, had risen to be a publishing magnate, making his initial fortune out of popular journalism, and had set up *Tit Bits* at the age of thirty. In 1891, he founded the publishers George Newnes Ltd and moved upmarket, launching a whole raft of illustrated magazines including, in 1897, *Country Life*. Newnes was the Liberal Member of Parliament for Swansea from 1890 to 1910, and was rewarded with a baronetcy on the grounds that he had pioneered decent popular literature. Lady Emily, wife of the architect Edwin Lutyens, painted a sympathetic portrait of him at the very moment in 1905 when his links with *Country Life* were to be severed:

> Sir George Newnes is such a dear man and I should like to get
> to know him privately ... Sir George has a nice open face with
> a keen blue eye, a good sort of radical and without any side or
> pretension, very kind, very cool headed and unemotional.

Hudson was to buy Newnes out the same year, establishing Country Life

(Previous page) Tortworth Court, Gloucestershire. The great house secure within its domain.

(Opposite) The creators of Country Life*: clockwise from top — Edward Hudson, founder and mastermind; Sir George Newnes, illustrated magazine millionaire; Gertrude Jekyll, high priestess of garden style; Sir Edwin Lutyens, architect of genius and the magazine's arbiter of taste; Sir Lawrence Weaver, advocate of the new; Lord Riddell, self-made publishing magnate — surrounding the magazine's first address at 10-11 Southampton Street, Strand, London.*

EDWARD HUDSON

LORD RIDDELL

SIR GEORGE NEWNES

SIR LAWRENCE WEAVER

GERTRUDE JEKYLL

SIR EDWIN LUTYENS

Ltd as an independent publishing company with Riddell on its board. George Allardice Riddell (1865-1934) had an even more meteoric career than Newnes and was from far humbler beginnings, being the son of a Brixton photographer. He was able to push his way up through the legal profession from nothing, making his fortune first as legal adviser and then as chairman of a Sunday sensational, *The News of the World*. Although his reputation was far from savoury, he was useful to Liberal governments, and a baronetcy and later a peerage came his way. He was virtually head of the Newnes publishing company, which was shortly to launch *Country Life*, and was also passionate about golf.

These men typify the energy and enterprise of late Victorian England. They were urban, commercial creatures, out to make their fortunes. So, too, was Edward Hudson (1854-1933) who dominated the first thirty-five years of the magazine's history. Bernard Darwin wrote: "The paper was the love of his life." He continues: "Mr. Hudson was always the controller of the paper's policy from the earliest days and as long as he lived."

Who was this extraordinary man who created what was to become a kind of minor national monument? The Hudsons were a Cumberland family who moved south to London where Edward's grandfather established the printing business of Hudson & Kearns. They lived on the wrong side of Hyde Park "in a gloomy mansion" and were solid trade with no great signs of social aspiration, Hudson starting work at fifteen in a firm of solicitors. That experience would have given him some common ground with Riddell, and, though uneducated, Hudson rose to the rank of chief conveyancing clerk before he took over the family firm at twenty-one. He lived with his unmarried sisters and an ailing brother, "fragile as porcelain", and only moved across the Park to 15 Queen Anne's Gate (where every room was "like a picture") when he was middle-aged. He is said to have formed a passion for country houses early in his life, riding out on his bicycle, or driving his invalid brother around in a car on his search for them.

Lytton Strachey, dipping his pen in its customary venom, described him as "a pathetically dreary figure ... a fish gliding underwater, and star-struck — looking up with his adoring eyes through his own dreadful element ... A kind of bourgeois gentilhomme also". Ralph Edwards, the furniture historian who worked on the magazine for a time, corroborates this view: "the very image of a prosperous British bourgeois, a typical minor Establishment figure". His manner was brusque and churlish except when — and this is revealing — he came into contact with the aristocracy when he assumed a manner of "extreme urbanity, verging on obsequiousness". Edwards goes on to tell us that he never wrote a line or read a book: "Uninterested in ideas, he had no general culture and strictly limited powers of conversation."

To Dora Carrington, whose brother, Noël, ran the book publishing side of the magazine for a time, he gave "the cold shudders". She saw him as "a gargoyle of a monstrosity". The only person who gives Hudson a sympathetic portrait is Edwin Lutyens' daughter, who records his kindness and good nature which she knew as a child (her sister, Ursula, was Hudson's god-daughter). Handsome he was not. "He was plain", Pamela Maude wrote, "with a large head and a long upper lip covered in a scrubby moustache. His arms hung at his side as though they were not needed." His protégé, Edwin Lutyens, put it another way: "Huddy [...] had no hands — in other words, he was a do-er not a maker." Devoid of sparkle and cripplingly shy, it was agony for him to speak in public. But he found solace in music and enjoyed a life-long friendship with the great cellist Madame Suggia to whom he gave a Stradivarius. In old age he married, Edwards acidly writes, a woman who tolerated his "many peculiarities".

Hudson was, however, a shrewd businessman. It was to be Riddell who led him into publishing, with a succession of new periodicals exploiting the innovation of quality illustration utilising the half-tone block which arose during the 1890s: *Famous Cricketers*, *The Army & Navy Gazette* and *Racing Illustrated*, the forerunner of *Country Life*. None of these indicate an aesthetic turn of mind, but Hudson had an unerring eye for quality in terms of print and paper and, above all, for block-making. These new magazines exploited developments in photography made during the 1880s which meant negatives could be produced more quickly and, due to the advent of the hand-held camera, opened up a far greater range of subject matter. This made possible art magazines such as *The Connoisseur* (1901) and *The Burlington Magazine* (1903). The notice announcing the launch of *Country Life* states that "the finest pictorial printing machinery obtainable which had been specially built in America for the production of the paper, has been imported ..."

The new magazine depended on three addresses, two of which were in Covent Garden: George Newnes' office in Southampton Street, from which the magazine was published and which handled the advertising, and the editorial office at 20 and 21 Tavistock Street, where the composing was done by hand, the editorial pages made up and the paper stored. When the magazine was finally assembled, it was taken by horse-van to Hudson & Kearns, the printers in Southwark Street across the river. The concern with quality production was to remain a hallmark of the magazine and, before 1914, was to lead to experiments in printing pages in tones of sepia and green and, in 1911, to the magazine's first colour plate.

Initially billed as *Country Life Illustrated incorporating Racing Illustrated*, the magazine could easily have come and gone. But by 1913, its status was

THE EDITORS
1958 TO PRESENT

JOHN ADAMS 1958-1973
MICHAEL WRIGHT 1973-1984
MARCUS BINNEY 1984-1986
JENNY GREENE 1986-1992
CLIVE ASLET 1993 -

such that the future Lord Runciman could bestow on it the accolade of being "the architectural conscience of the nation". However it would be hard to give such credit to its first issue which had as its frontispiece the avuncular and portly Earl of Suffolk and Berkshire fondling a monocle. Out of its twenty-eight pages, ten were devoted to racing, three to staghounds, two to cattle, four to the Princess of Wales' dogs, with a paragraph 'On the Green' and a golfing story. Only two pages bearing the heading 'Country Homes: Baddesley Clinton' provided any hint of what was to come.

In its early months, the magazine appealed to fashionable society and probably had a predominantly female readership. The frontispiece quickly became a society portrait; regular features appeared on fashion; 'Town Topics' covered the round of the *haute monde* and there was much space devoted to dogs. The majority of the magazine's pages, however, was given over to various sporting activities, particularly those embodied by Ascot, Henley or the Varsity Sports. Regular columns including 'Country Notes', 'Books of the Day' and 'In the Garden', together with an abundance of nature photographs, established the long-term future of the magazine.

Ten years later, in 1907, the magazine was very different. Its layout was far more accomplished, with striking headpieces by James Byam Shaw, some of which were to be used until 1939. 'Town Topics' had gone and, apart from theatre reviews, the magazine assumed a firm country focus consisting of three subjects which persisted throughout the magazine's history: a celebration of nature as seen in the landscape or wildlife or seasonal toil;

(Right) The first picture of a country house in the magazine: Baddesley Clinton, Warwickshire, 1897.

20

an exploration of domestic architecture and gardens with the weekly article on 'Country Homes' as its focal point; and a wealth of sporting coverage from falconry to fox-hunting.

From the outset, the magazine's impact had been primarily visual rather than literary. Even today, *Country Life* is looked at more often than read, a consequence of the expertise of the magazine's photographers. Hudson probably acted as some kind of picture editor, and Edwards described Hudson sitting in his office looking at every picture, rejecting half of them. This was his redeeming feature, for he not only set the magazine's visual style, but was to be responsible for selecting some of the most haunting images of a lost world, the golden dream of Edwardian England. Whether it is a ploughman pushing his solitary furrow across a field, a frosted wood, a room in some ancient mansion or an aristocrat with her children, every picture exudes a lyrical romanticism. However varied the subjects, the magazine visually reads as one and that could only have been achieved by the control of a single discerning eye.

Hudson was fortunate in securing the services of two great photographers who established the magazine's style. The first was Charles Latham (died *c*.1909), an architectural photographer of note during the 1890s. He was a workaday man from Balham who dropped the letter 'h' and was referred to as "the lame photographer". But he was a genius with the camera lens, transforming country houses in the way society photographers transfigured the aristocratic ladies on the magazine's frontispiece. Christopher Hussey, who was to succeed Hudson as the dominant influence on the

(Left) Henry Avray Tipping in one of his gardens.

magazine, recorded that as early as 1903 Latham was beginning to denude the interiors of country houses of their Victorian clutter, presenting instead rooms with "a few perfectly placed and apposite furnishings. Indeed one chair, placed askew in the foreground facing a fireplace, virtually became his signature". These "re-arrangements" coincided with the arrival of a new contributor, Henry Avray Tipping, more of whom below.

The second photographer was the internationally-renowned Frederick Evans (1853-1945), who was saluted by the great American photographer Alfred Stieglitz as "the greatest exponent of architectural photography". Like Latham, he was a master of manipulation and owed something in his approach to buildings to the French Impressionists. He would wait for days for a particular effect of light and, like Latham, was quite capable of repositioning furnishings to achieve a perfect shot, even though Hudson hardly ever allowed him to photograph an English country house. Evans' most memorable series of pictures were of French chateaux, a series which ran from 1906 until the outbreak of war in 1914. Although superb, their subject matter sits awkwardly within the brief of *Country Life*. His earlier series of cathedrals and East Anglian church interiors are closer to the heart of the magazine: empty spaces bathed in shafts of luminous light; textured stone and wood; weathered walls and roof beams. Latham and Evans are the photographic giants but their work accompanied pictures by a large number of other Edwardian photographers similarly inspired by the shifting radiances common to the English pictorial landscape tradition epitomised by Turner and Constable.

The influence of some of the first text contributors lasted well beyond their own active involvement in the magazine. The earliest of these, and by far the most famous, was probably Gertrude Jekyll (1843-1932), whom Hudson met around 1899 and whose book *Wood and Garden* was reviewed in the March issue of that year. Jekyll was already an established figure in the gardening world, and for thirty years she contributed to *Country Life* in the main 'Garden Notes', occasionally writing on particular houses. She was to become a landmark in the history of twentieth-century gardening with a profound feeling for nature and every aspect of garden craft. Endowed with a painter's eye for colour and form, she lifted gardening to the status of a fine art. Through Jekyll, Hudson met the young Edwin Lutyens, whom he instantly commissioned to build Deanery Garden, his first country house at Sonning. Jekyll laid out the garden, achieving a perfect resolution of formal and naturalistic styles.

There is something intriguing about the Jekyll, Lutyens and Hudson trio. Although she was an apostle of the Arts and Crafts Movement, Jekyll was a member of the landed classes. Lutyens, like Hudson, came from out-

(Opposite) The staircase at Château La Rochefoucauld photographed by Frederick Evans. In the years before 1914 he took a superb series of photographs of French chateaux.

THE ENGLISH ARCADIA

(Opposite) Farm buildings at Poxwell Manor,
Dorset. The debt to Constable and his
successors is apparent.

side this elite but his marriage to an earl's daughter, Lady Emily Lytton,
gained him social acceptability. Lady Emily had no time for Hudson
despite the fact that he was to prove an invaluable ally in promoting her
husband's work. Hudson worshipped Lutyens and one wonders whether he
owed his visual education to him. Lutyens' office was next door to his house
in Queen Anne's Gate, and he helped Hudson in arranging it and
Lindisfarne Castle, his northern home. Lutyens wrote in 1908, that when
staying there he spent his time "looking, arranging furniture, flowers" for
the visit of the Princess of Wales, an awkward encounter over which
Hudson was "dreadfully nervous". In 1905 Lutyens designed the magazine's
new offices to look, as one author has remarked, like a slice of Hampton
Court in the midst of Covent Garden Market. The architect Paul Paget
wrote: "the presiding genii [of *Country Life*] were a triumvirate consisting of
Edward Hudson in supreme control, Edwin Lutyens the final arbiter of
taste and Lord Riddell, the mastermind in matters of the Press …"

If Hudson was outclassed socially and aesthetically by Jekyll and
Lutyens, the same was true of another key figure whose influence on the
magazine's direction was to be definitive — Henry Avray Tipping (1855-
1929). Ralph Edwards describes how Tipping would burst into the
boardroom reducing Hudson immediately to the status of "an obedient
slave". In Hudson's eyes, Tipping, like Lutyens, was "a veritable oracle". He
was landed gentry, had independent means and moved with ease in London
society. At his country house in Gwent he even entertained the Prime
Minister. At Oxford, he went through an aesthete phase, wearing his hair
long and sporting an oversize flower in his button hole. However, he took a
first in Modern History in 1878 and began his working career on *The
Dictionary of National Biography*. He was passionate about the theatre and
gardens, creating and designing a succession of them.

He was a strong personality who refused to be crossed and always got his
own way. One suspects that when he and Hudson visited country houses for
inclusion in the magazine, Hudson must have been the passenger of the
two. Tipping's earliest signed articles on country houses appear in 1907 but
he was writing for the magazine four years earlier. Darwin wrote with perception that "he was the first to apply the methods of historical research to
the subject" and his articles were genuine contributions to architectural history, bringing the country house and garden centre-stage within the
magazine.

The only other architectural writer with an impact comparable to Tipping was Sir Lawrence Weaver (1876-1930). Weaver was a very different character with very different tastes. He was a self-made man and owed his education to his mother, who taught the piano. Although he had some training in an architect's office he began his working life as a commercial traveller dealing in builder's ironmongery. He thus became fascinated by leadwork and from 1906 wrote a series of articles on the topic which led to him being taken on as architectural editor four years later. Although Hudson had been an earnest advocate of Lutyens' work, the magazine showed little commitment to contemporary architecture.

Weaver was to change all that in the six years he was with the magazine until called to wartime service. Under his aegis, there appeared a series of articles on the architecture and restoration of country houses called 'Lesser Country Houses of Today and Yesterday', and he also produced, under the magazine's imprint, a series of books on the design, construction and repair of small houses and cottages. With his enthusiam, *Country Life* championed architects associated with the Arts and Crafts Movement, and it sponsored architectural competitions with informed architectural critique. He, more than anyone else, earned the magazine's accolade, bestowed on it in 1913, as "the keeper of the architectural conscience of the nation".

Weaver provided a strong counterpoint to Tipping, for he was a man with "strong religious, puritanical and philanthropic convictions" with a commitment after the war to disabled ex-sevicemen. Under the patronage of Lord Lee, he was to embark on a highly successful career which brought him a knighthood through his commitment to public service and new industrial design. His brilliant career was cut short at fifty-three by a heart attack, but his value to *Country Life* was inestimable.

The magazine's interest in antiques, which represented potential advertising revenue, was signalled as early as August 1899 with the first of a series of articles by Gerald Metcalfe. However, Margaret Jourdain (1876-1951), who began to write for the magazine at least as early as 1906, was to become indelibly associated with the subject. The impoverished daughter of a clergyman, and herself an early Oxford graduate, she was self-taught as far as her knowledge of the decorative arts was concerned. She churned out pieces on lace, samplers, stumpwork, wallpaper, plasterwork and furniture virtually to order. James Lees-Milne painted a memorable picture of her:

> Margaret Jourdain was squat, broad, and plain. Dressed in clothes subfusc she favoured large hats with rampageous feathers. At the end of a long gold chain she carried a Georgian spy-glass which she applied in a rather menacing manner to a small, beady eye.

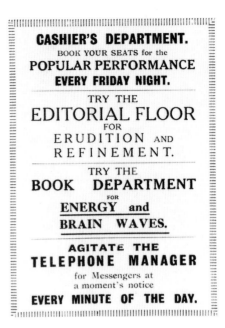

(Above) A humourous advertisement put together by the magazine's production team for a staff party in 1920.

(Opposite) One of Weaver's 'Lesser Country Houses of Today'. The garden of Little Boarhunt recently laid out by H. Inigo Triggs. Such pictures spread new styles.

A pioneer in her day, she is more remembered today for her long liaison with the novelist Ivy Compton-Burnet into whose flat she moved in October 1919. Ralph Edwards was to review her novels as an act of charity in *Country Life* deeming them "unhealthy". In the early days, Margaret Jourdain was the celebrity, attracting to herself a swarm of young men. Caustic, categorical, acidly witty and argumentative, she moved in a world of journalists, museum officials, collectors and decorators. But her steady stream of books opened up fields of research, resurrecting major figures in the history of the arts, such as William Kent.

The other contributor in the antiques field was Percy Macquoid (1852-1925), whose articles started in 1911 and lasted until his death. A friend of Tipping, he shared a love for the theatre in which he worked as a designer on a long series of productions for both Sir Beerbohm Tree and Sir George Alexander. He was also a collector with a flair for interior decoration: the house he built at Bayswater had each room furnished in a different period. Macquoid owed his luxurious lifestyle to a rich wife. Harold Peto, the garden designer and another friend of Tipping's, had been his best man. What began as a career producing archaeologically-correct period sets in the theatre led to a life-long pioneering study *The History of English Furniture* (1904-1908), a landmark achievement signalled by Tipping in the pages of the magazine: "Mr Macquoid was the first serious student to bestow time and attention on the comprehensive survey of the field …" In 1923, Hudson asked Macquoid to put the material into dictionary form.

All the same, it is notable how many of the articles in the magazine's early issues did not have a byline. Surprisingly, that feeling of anonynimity extends to the editors who hardly take on any character at all.

The first, J. E. Vincent, was soon succeeded by Peter Anderson Graham who occupied the position for thirty years and who wrote vast tracks of the magazine including the leader, 'Country Notes', 'Agricultural Notes' and 'The Book of the Week'. He is recorded as "a leisurely man of letters rather than a working journalist", a dignified, unpretentious figure in baggy country clothes.

The variety of subject-matter covered by the magazine engendered substantial advertising revenue during a period when the commercial potential of the half-tone block as an illustrative medium was also being realised. Darwin wrote, matter-of-factly:

> I think that it can firmly be said that it has performed a special service during all those years, to those who are interested in buying or selling such things as furniture and pictures, motor-cars and all kinds of agricultural equipment.

Above all, it benefited the property market, represented initially by a modest two pages, gradually expanding to form a major feature of every issue of the magazine.

But even that does not account for the magazine's quite extraordinary success, which is all the more surprising considering that Edward Hudson, the originator of *Country Life*, was, according to Darwin: "not by upbringing a country man, and had not, I think, any great familiarity with many of the things which came naturally to those who are country bred ..."

Perhaps the answer is provided by the historian of Knight, Frank and Rutley: "Hudson glamourised the country, made successful businessmen long to live in it, secure in the knowledge that by selling up and buying land one became at least a sort of gentleman."

This glamorous vision is echoed by Hudson's own life, as he progressed from a country house built for him by Lutyens in the vernacular style, and from there to a restored castle at Lindisfarne, and then finally to a genuine old manor house, Plumpton Place, in Sussex.

(Above) Lutyens' offices for Country Life *brought a taste of Wren's Hampton Court to a narrow site in the middle of Covent Garden, central London.*

Lytton Strachey gave a rare picture of how Hudson lived his dream. Strachey was asked to a house party at Lindisfarne Castle in September 1918. Although the siting of the castle was "magnificent", he had little to say in favour of Lutyens' work on it: "very dark, with nowhere to sit, and nothing but stone under, over and round you ..."

The other guests give an insight into the social milieu of *Country Life's* founder: there was Madame Suggia, the cellist, by whom Strachey was enslaved; a cosmopolitan Jewess, Lady Lewis; a couple of uncultured rich Americans, the husband playing the banjo; Suggia's mother ("a subject in itself for a Balzac novel") and her accompanist; the publisher, William Heinemann; and a Mr and Mrs Fort, "Mr. F. ... with a voice like a megaphone ..." Strachey was stranded there for a whole week.

More than any other magazine, *Country Life* was to become the manual of gentrification for the late Victorian and Edwardian middle classes. It was created at a crucial period in the formation of the attitudes and ideas which were to dominate British society well into the twentieth century.

At the time when the landowning classes lost their political and social power, they were to retain their cultural hegemony over society through the projection of their culture as the model way of living for the aspiring middle classes. By the 1880s, over eighty percent of the population was urban-based, and one might have thought that towns and cities were where future aspirations should logically have been focused.

Instead, they centred around a totally new vision of rural life, part of a phenomenon which we now recognise as an invented tradition. We must now consider how this fiction was created.

An Arcadian Vision

"It started with a title that falls like music on the ear", states the article celebrating the twenty-fifth anniversary of *Country Life* on 7th January 1922, "ours being an island race whereof even the town dweller is a country man at heart". By then, everything in the magazine was seen to embody the quintessence of English ideals. It is significant that such a simple statement could not have been made forty years earlier. But then a revolution as to what constituted national identity had since occurred.

In 1897, the year of the Diamond Jubilee and the launch of the magazine, Britain dominated the world through its industrial achievement in a century of dramatic change. Its towns and cities, reinvigorated by the Industrial Revolution, offered handsome public buildings and parks, gracious suburbs and vibrant shopping streets as well as a darker side: factory life, slum dwellings, pollution, disease and poverty. It was to be these negative aspects which were to influence the late Victorian urbanite, unleashing a strong reaction against urban centres which were no longer viewed as triumphant monuments to a technological revolution providing enormous wealth, but rather as embodiments of false ideals and sordid vulgarity. In addition, the teeming proletariat within these cities could represent a social and political threat to the affluent professional classes as the struggle between labour and capital entered a turbulent and bitter phase.

The view that life in the countryside offered a positive alternative to that led in the city was advanced by prominent writers and thinkers such as John Ruskin, for whom technology, capitalism and industrial society represented the antithesis of the good life which could be found in the order and tranquillity of the countryside. In drawing this conclusion, Ruskin (and others) were following a long literary tradition, one with which every public-school educated reader of *Country Life* would have been familiar: the *beatus vir* of classical times, the fortunate man who found contentment away from the anxious and decadent life of the city, in a quiet rural abode where he could cultivate the stoic virtues of simplicity, independence and equanimity. This tradition had been reinterpreted by the landscape movement of the eighteenth century, when tracts of countryside around great houses had been rearranged to create hills and lakes and planted with trees to form pictorial vistas. These physical manifestations of literary Elysian fields drew their inspiration from the descriptions of landscape found in the pastoral poetry of antiquity, where nymphs and shepherds blissfully passed their time in sylvan glades bathed in an eternal golden light. This paradisal landscape was celebrated by the Latin poet Virgil in his *Eclogues*, and visualised in painting by the seventeenth-century French artist Claude Lorraine.

(Opposite) The Arcadian ideal. The pool at Garsington Manor, Garsington, near Oxford, designed by Charles Mallows for Lady Ottoline Morrell.

It is ironic, but perhaps understandable, that the countryside of late Victorian Britain was increasingly reinvented in terms of this ancient tradition by those living in its cities: the quest for innovation and invention, the very qualities which had made the nation economically great, were replaced by values which redefined the English spirit in terms of the preservation of the status quo and the celebration of the harmony supposedly offered by rural life. Conservatism and a suspicion of change began to pervade society, which found a creative expression for these values in a largely fictional view of the countryside, where ancient stoic virtues were seen to flourish, ones which put a premium on the slow-moving, the stable and domestic. After decades of massive economic and social change, these alternative attributes quickly assumed an aura of spiritual authority and consequently underpinned a new sense of collective identity from which the attributes of industrialised society were excluded. Of course, this idyllic, unchanging vision of the countryside was far removed from the shifting realities facing the countryside during the Georgian and Victorian eras. It had, in fact, been the setting for radical change as the landscape was dramatically altered by the property enclosures of rural landlords, the agricultural revolution and the ravages caused by the exploitation of natural resources which lurked beneath the earth's surface. Much of this rural revolution, which included

(Above) 'Good Worksmanship': the eternal ploughman at his task. The cruel realities of agricultural depression and rural poverty found little place in the magazine.

(Opposite) 'Three Worthy People': no issue was complete without its romantic glimpses of rural toil accompanied by a whimsical caption.

(Previous page) Bibury, Oxfordshire. The village romanticised.

(Above) The Trinity Foot Beagles at Reaveley: every issue celebrated the hunt and the shoot.

the creation of our present field system with its hedgerows and clumps of trees, has, ironically, become regarded in our own century as a precious part of our landscape heritage.

Nonetheless, the ideal of rural living was a powerful one, for it provided a ready-made encapsulation of the hierarchical values that reflected the social aspirations of the professional and urban-based classes who made up the the major part of the readership of *Country Life*. The life of a country gentleman was seen as particularly desirable, and the magazine provided, week by week, a pantheon of images that gradually formed a powerfully enticing illustration of national identity: portraits of members of old families, ancient manor houses and gardens, views of an unspoiled landscape depicted through the seasons, ordinary countrymen at their toil and the gentry engaging in country pursuits. The overwhelming impression one received when turning the pages of the magazine was (and still is) of continuity and tradition. These values crossed ideological divisions and were adopted with equal fervour by Socialist and Tory voter alike, since both political persuasions looked back beyond what they came to regard as the horrendous blot of the Industrial Revolution to an imaginary rural England. The Socialist could thus conjure up a lost countryside in which the honest craftsman had practised his skills and passed his life within the security of an unchanging village community, while the Tory could envisage an age when the social hierarchy lay undisturbed, guided by the landed classes who dominated local affairs as their natural right. The conceptual framework of *Country Life* was almost the answer to a national prayer.

The facts behind the popular appeal of this selective and fictional reading of rural values seem only to contradict its paradoxical success. *Country Life* apotheosised a lifestyle and culture of what was essentially a defeated class — the aristocracy and gentry of pre-industrialised Britain. Its launch in 1897 was but thirteen years after the end of aristocratic government, symbolised by the Third Reform Act of 1883-1884. This had extended the franchise to the working classes, the first time that the vote was disassociated from some kind of property qualification. This went hand-in-hand with the agricultural depression of the 1880s, an erosion of the financial basis of the landed classes which lasted until 1945. Death duties were introduced in 1894 at 8%, but it was to be the People's Budget of 1909 that was to bite particularly deep. Income tax rose to 1s. 2d. in the pound, a supertax for those with incomes in excess of £3,000 per annum was introduced and death duties increased to 15%. The landed classes fought back but it was to be a losing battle. Their political power was finally lost with the passing of the Parliament Act of 1910, which rendered the House of Lords virtually

(Below) The Cattistock Pack in 1906. One of few countryside images which remain unchanged.

(Next page) Three upper class young women enjoying nature in Burnham Beeches, a photograph which was not used.

impotent. The rapid erosion of power in the provinces as the new county and district councils took over only continued the rot. The 1914-1918 war was to do the rest.

The decline of the aristocratic infrastructure would, it might seem, have made its visible focus — the country house — redundant. But if the aristocracy's political and social power declined, its cultural influence did not: the rural aristocratic lifestyle was what the new rich from the commercial and professional classes aspired to experience. This cultural shift was nothing unusual for families which had made fortunes in trade and commerce from Tudor times onwards, and then built country houses, setting themselves up as country gentlemen.

This was never more true than during the Victorian era. The difference was that by the 1890s, it did not make economic sense to establish a rural power base, since landowning had ceased to be a passport to power. The new generation of landed estate owners were living according to a new shared collective cultural ideal, where the English country squire, whose pursuit of leisure, commitment to political service and cultivation of style set the highest standards within the framework provided by the country house and garden.

The making of money and the unpleasant manual aspects of industrial production had no place in this idyllic system. The professional classes — lawyers, doctors, public officials, journalists and men of letters — tried to cast themselves according to a model of gentry living which had become increasingly economically and politically redundant.

Such a profound shift in social attitudes inevitably produced its own literature. Writing about the country emerged as a genre during the 1890s and in 1904, The *Manchester Guardian* became the first national newspaper to establish a "Country Diary" column. By that date "Country Notes" was a well established feature of *Country Life*. Such pieces were written with an urban audience in mind, one which had little idea of the realities of rural life. "For the past ten years", wrote the German cultural attaché to London Hermann Mathesius in a section of his book *Das Englische Haus* (1904-1905) entitled 'New Move to the Country', "there has been a very active market towards a close contact with nature. A number of excellent journals dealing in detail with everything connected with life in the country have begun publication."

Of these, *Country Life* was to be by far the most influential and enduring, and its creator, Edward Hudson, was acutely aware of the business potential to be exploited in matching and furthering the mood of the period. One can have no doubt that he, like everyone else at the time, believed in it all. But then he also knew how to paint a picture of the Arcadian ideal.

Role-playing

Two things enabled city-dwellers' enjoyment of country life to take off: the increase in leisure time, and developments in transport. The professional classes had expanded enormously by 1900, and the nation was hugely prosperous. Renting a place for the family in the country or at the seaside was the norm for an annual holiday throughout the Victorian period. Progressing to having a permanent second home or commuting daily in order to escape the polluted atmosphere of the city was made possible first by the railways and then increasingly by the advent of the motor car. The life conjured up in the pages of *Country Life* was made particularly accessible for those with a motor car. 'On the Road' first appeared as a regular column in 1899 and by 1914, under the title of 'The Motoring World', it sometimes occupied as many as twenty pages in any single issue, excluding the amount of space in the advertising pages. The Automobile Club of Great Britain and Ireland was founded the same year as the magazine, and its members included four peers of the realm and eighty-five gentlemen of means. Motoring was exclusive, recreation for the rich, calling for expensive vehicles, accomodation in which to house them, special clothes and even a new type of servant, the chauffeur. In 1896, the Light Locomotives on Highways Act raised the speed limit to 14 m.p.h., and this was raised again in 1903 to 25 m.p.h. All those comfortable new houses in the Home Counties published in *Country Life* could thus be easily reached. The magazine and the motor car were to be inextricably linked from here on.

Leisure, wealth and the motor car meant that in the two decades preceding 1914, villages all over the country were facing invasion. The car brought with it people whose idea of what the country represented was very different to that understood by the indigenous population. The car-owners were to purchase houses which had belonged to ancient families, build new ones or transform cottages, adding every modern convenience. These peoples' notion of the "simple life" bore no relation to that lived by those who toiled on the land: what brought them there was primarily the pursuit of pleasure and sport, even if it meant morris-dancing themselves.

The magazine's attempts to come to grips with "genuine" country people reveal its singular value system. Few issues up to 1914 are without stage-managed tableaux, in which a few humble villagers are tastefully arranged in the village inn or caught gathering blossom for the May Day revels. The debt to seventeenth-century scenes of low life of the kind painted by Ostade and Teniers is obvious. Rural types are presented to the reader as specimens worthy of study, displayed with the same attention usually devoted to animals and insects. A rare incursion into a workhouse in 1911

(Top right) The droll headpiece for the motoring pages — showing a putto wearing a chauffeur's cap — celebrates motoring as a new adventure for the upper classes.

(Lower right) Entitled 'The Return', a caption formerly reserved for the return of the hunt to the manor house. This photograph, taken in 1902, shows the novel mode of transport.

THE AUTOMOBILE WORLD

enabled an encounter with a ward of decrepit and poverty-stricken elderly countrywomen. But the writer tells us:

> I never weary of hearing about old customs, old beliefs, cures and charms ... or, greatest pleasure of all ... their old ballads, songs and dance tunes. The dear old face of the woman in bed broke into dimpling laughter as she told me how her village wake was kept in her youth ... I hum a few bars, and the old head nods and the fingers beat to the lilt of them ...

This poor bedridden wretch was but a picturesque token of the folk culture of pre-industrial Britain, which offered a more palatable alternative to the urban working-class culture symbolised by the gin-palace and the music-hall and, by that date, ragtime and the cinema. Before 1914, villages and their old folk represented a kind of living history, survivors from an age when rural communities had consisted of sturdy, simple, deferential folk, in whom the spiritual values of "Old England" — order, harmony and tradition — resided. The 1890s witnessed a quest for the folk songs and dances of rural popular culture, which had almost been lost. By 1900, *Country Life*, with a steady flow of articles on English villages, old estate servants and rural crafts, firmly supported this notion of a lost rural world.

Both the buildings and inhabitants in these articles appear in much the same way as Thomas Hardy characterised them in his novels. Old country customs — ranging from May Day to harvest rituals — most of which had been suppressed by the Victorians on grounds of cruelty, immorality or superstition, were now brushed down, sanitised and revived under the aegis of the invading middle classes bent on reinstating a fictional "Merry England". The pages of *Country Life* are witness to this celebration of the virtues of vernacular architecture and of pre-industrial handicraft. Such a folk revival fitted in exactly with the tenets of the Arts and Crafts Movement which reacted against industrialisation and the city. The Movement's practitioners, among them C. R. Ashbee, W. R. Lethaby and Ernest Gimson, fled capitalist centres of commerce and set up workshops in the Cotswolds to produce handicrafts. *Country Life* was to feature houses designed by its own architects and Gertrude Jekyll, the prime gardening correspondent, belonged firmly within its orbit. Although the magazine did not yet actively embrace the conservationist's cause, the picture coverage accorded to topics as varied as old almshouses, Oxford and Cambridge colleges, old barns and shop fronts, emphasises its role at the inception of the preservation movement: the foundation of The Society for the Protection of Ancient Buildings in 1877; the passing of the Ancient Monuments Protection Act in 1882; and in 1895, the creation of The National Trust. These were to be areas in which the magazine left its mark.

THE DOG

ANIMAL PORTRAITS ASSUMED A STATUS EQUAL TO THOSE OF SOCIETY LADIES IN THE MAGAZINE. TWO CAMEO HEADS ILLUSTRATED AN ARTICLE IN 1911 BY LADY SYBIL GRANT ON 'PYRENEAN MOUNTAIN DOGS'.

(Opposite) Aristocracy beatified. The Marchioness of Granby with her child, later Lady Diana Cooper.

(Right) Cockle gatherers at Stiffkey, Norfolk, women borne down by their load, walk towards the sunset.

The fertility of rural produce did, however, provide a suitably bountiful picture of the countryside: by 1914, two-thirds of working land had gone over to some form of market gardening, supplying milk, eggs, fruit, vegetables, livestock and its produce to towns and cities. In 1899, there were two series in the magazine — 'Profitable Poultry' and 'Flower and Fruit Farms of Great Britain'. Photographs of the pedigree herds of the aristocracy came to resemble society portraits. On *Country Life*'s twenty-fifth anniversary, one writer stated, during what was a period of considerable agricultural depression: "The tractor plough received its send-off in these columns, and there is scarcely a new invention in drainage, in river cleaning, in machinery of any kind that has not been illustrated and explained."

Although *Country Life* promoted a beguiling picture of leisurely engagement with the countryside, it had little interest in the tough reality of rural living. Even in 1914, life was still hard, and women laboured in the fields where they could, taking in laundry and needlework to make ends meet, and their menfolk toiled long hours for very little. Only by 1918 did children cease to work part of the day at harvest time, for the 1870 Education Act had had little impact. It is now noticeable how condescending the attitude of the classes which read *Country Life* was towards those working in the country. For them, the countryside represented leisure rather than toil, and the opportunity to indulge in another late Victorian obsession, the cult of sport. The pages given over to sport exceed in number those devoted to any other topic. This is of fundamental importance for understanding the success of the magazine, for when it started in 1897, the role of sport as a common pastime binding the old landed classes and the new aspiring ones was fairly recent. An editorial in 1899, prompted by that year's Varsity Sports, by then a fashionable occasion, is revealing:

> But it is not only in athletic sports ... that the public interest has grown from nil to its present proportions during Queen Victoria's reign. Of every outdoor game the history is the same — cricket, football, golf, what you will — all were utterly disregarded fifty or sixty years ago ... it is scarcely to be doubted that the general results are good — good for the health of the nation, and in living witnesses to its results in the persons of strong sons and tall daughters. Nor are there lacking instances to show that athletic and intellectual success can go hand-in-hand.

A revolution in social atitudes occurred, in which sport was adapted and regulated to embody principles of self-control and energetic competition. The cult of sport originated in public schools where it was used to maintain

(Left) George Head, aged 86, still in service after 55 years on the Broadlands estate, Hampshire.

(Above) Golf as a new fashionable pastime.

discipline, to reflect a ready response to command and to instil a sense of community spirit. It defined masculinity, exalting physical bravery and prowess above intellectual attributes, combining a cult of individual achievement with the cohesion inherent in team activities — all mirroring the virtues of public life. Sport could be played by the stockbroker as well as the squire: all it called for was money and leisure. This was the age of the gentleman amateur.

By 1900, the old traditional aristocratic sports of hunting, shooting and fishing were joined by a huge list of new activities. In every issue, numerous articles were devoted to hunting, shooting, falconry, cricket, tennis, bicycling, fishing, golf, racing, rowing and polo. A series on 'Sport in Other Lands' found the intrepid British sportsman circling the globe to massacre any form of wildlife from Bosnia to Ceylon, from India to Somaliland. Regular occasions like Ascot, the University Boat Race, Henley Regatta and the Eton and Harrow Match, all feature. Sports emphasised class distinctions. "Coarse" fishing was lower class; "game" fishing was upper.

THE ENGLISH ARCADIA

Owning racehorses was another way up the social ladder, and since the railways meant that horses could travel, the sport boomed. It even had a regular column, 'Between the Flags', as did golf, 'On the Green', again the prerogative of the well-heeled. The professional golfer was tolerated but not accepted as a social equal. Rowing was exclusive, with its clubs and boathouses along the Thames: sports like bicycling and tennis, which quickly percolated down the social scale, were dropped.

Country Life is still published every Thursday, in time for what was then another relatively new and spreading phenomenon — the weekend. In earlier periods, the country house was occupied at certain seasons of the year with a massive decampment to London for the Season during the frenetically busy summer months.

Since the eighteenth century, there had been house-parties in the country but with the advent of the railways, and then the car, visits for relatively short periods became an increasing possibility and the weekend stay-away was born. An entry in Lady Cynthia Asquith's diary for Friday 30th April 1915 catches the new rhythm: "Mr Norton and Countess Beckendorff arrived teatime, having motored from London and seen several churches on their way."

With the five-day week now the norm for the professional classes, the weekend habit rapidly grew. It was to produce a new kind of house, which expanded and contracted in response to weekenders. *Country Life* was precisely the right type of magazine for this new market, and no country house drawing room was complete without its copy for guests to savour.

(Above) Blue Gown and Brindle at the Kennel Club in 1898.

(Left) The gentlemanly ritual of the duel was kept alive through fencing, as here at Harrow School.

The Country House

Much of the fame of *Country Life* rests on its long series of articles on country houses. Indeed, this series established the country house as the central icon of the idyllic vision promulgated by the magazine, an icon which remains as evocative a century on. The magazine's first issue featured a short article on a moated Tudor manor house, Baddesley Clinton, which was accompanied by a haunting photograph.

In 1916, Avray Tipping, who by then wrote the majority of feature articles, used the occasion of the thousandth issue to muse about the magazine's treatment of country houses. He noted that when the magazine was launched, the treatment of country houses had had to be "tentative". The ground was certainly fertile for a detailed consideration of them, he wrote, but, in a curious turn of phrase, one had to "begin homeopathically and only increase the dose as the tonic gave strength to the reader's system …" The response to this doctor's medicine was rapid. "It has succeeded", he went on to say, "in being educative without being pedantic, informing yet attractive … each one has been so treated as to show some merit, teach some lesson, and exercise some influence on the taste of today." Tipping then proceeded to give a highly personal account of English architectural history in which every period radiated glory, except for the Victorian era when the country house was "allowed to stray on to very unsatisfactory lines". Harlaxton and Knebworth are held up as: "The extinction of a living style and an ignorant copying of every age and nation …" The aim of the articles was to give "hint and guidance to the many who propose to build or enlarge or re-do their habitations and their gardens".

Tipping's articles did not only educate the public in what he regarded as good architectural taste, they also supplied a great deal of local history. Ralph Edwards has left us a picture of Tipping surrounded by genealogical reference books, for each article was not only about the house but also its family and history. Where a new family purchased or restored a decaying house, the family history of its earlier occupants was grafted on to that of the present owners, a trend consistent with the values of continuity and stability central to the era. Latham's photographs complemented these attitudes with excellent precision: people rarely feature in them, and if there is someone, it is only a lady with a parasol, bestowing on them a sense of timelessness. Although Latham's camera lens presents a romanticised and glamourised picture, he, in common with the Victorian tradition of architectural photography, always maintained a clarity of volume and a detailed eye for the materials of construction. Vista was another dominant ingredient, the use of perspective leading the eye either to or away from the house,

(Opposite) Eaton Hall, Cheshire. Many of the early houses covered by Country Life *were of the solid mid-Victorian style which the magazine was soon to disown.*

the picture's tonality softening into the distance. Lighting was ingeniously
manipulated to cast shadows which could either emphasise built form or
dapple the area below as it percolated down through canopies of leaves. No
opportunity for exploiting water reflections is ever lost, be they found on a
lake, canal or through a fountain. Significantly, there are no winter pictures,
so that the country house seems only to bask in a sunlit reverie, creating an
overwhelming sense of serenity and stillness.

The elegiac quality of Latham's photographs only masked an awareness
by those running the magazine of the inevitable passing of the old aristocratic order. An editorial in 1905 states:

> It is difficult to overrate the encouragement given to residents
> in all parts of England during the long years of agricultural
> depression by the steady support which the historic families of
> this country, those who united political power with territorial
> possessions, gave to the impoverished rural districts by refusing
> to close the great houses.

Five years later in 1910, another editorial returns to the subject, bemoan-
ing the break up of the great estates due to the depression:

> ... the impoverished owners of land were in a very large num-
> ber of cases unable to keep up the houses and estates to which

*(Above) 'Gaffer and gammer', an idealised
image of country folk in 1909.*

*(Opposite) Photograph recently discovered in
the archive taken c. 1900, thought to be of
Kelmarsh Hall.*

they had been accustomed. Hundreds were left empty and allowed to fall into half ruinous condition. Others were let to sporting tenants and other strangers. A complete revolution was brought about in rural England.

Those who perused the property pages of the magazine would have been more than aware of this. Great houses were advertised to be let for shooting parties and there was a steady stream of houses for sale. The landowners who survived these changes were those with incomes from industry, the City or urban rents. But the country house, once a power base, was becoming something very different. Until the landed classes lost their political power, the country house had been run by the owner who not only farmed the land around it but who also controlled one or more parliamentary seats, or found himself sitting in the House of Lords. As lord lieutenant of the county or even as a Justice of the Peace, he was the arm of government in the counties. Rights of presentation to benefices ensured that the church was also firmly bound in as part of the system. The great house offered employment to those servants within it or to the huge staff needed to maintain its gardens and stables. Bit by bit this pre-eminence was to be eroded. Those owners who could transformed their country houses into homes in the country. Where landed families had more than one house on the estate, they retrenched and moved into the smaller. To the aspiring middle classes, such a house in the country, however modest in its new guise, offered not only social status but a genuine retreat from the cares of office life and the social round of London.

From the outset, the display of country houses in *Country Life* represented an extremely lucrative marketing vehicle. The articles celebrating them for embodying the virtues of pre-industrial Old England were matched by advertisements offering them for sale. It was the perfect commercial marriage. While the magazine's editors might lament the demise of the old order, the publication's own prosperity depended on it purveying achievable dreams to those who aspired to recreate it. The magazine's articles and images wove a tissue of romantic associations, tranquillity, beauty, dignity and tradition. Lord Lee of Fareham, who was to play an important role in advancing the career of Lawrence Weaver, recalls how the allure of the magazine's property pages had even reached Canada : "... an intoxicating range of temptations in the shape of English country houses — Tudor,

(Above) The motor car called for a new kind
of outdoor servant, the chauffeur, and a special
uniform which drew on both military and
domestic livery models.

Jacobean, Georgian and whatnot — which were at the disposal of any lovesick exile who could make a fortune and retire to his native land." This is precisely what Lee did in purchasing Chequers, for which he employed Avray Tipping to lay out the garden, before eventually leaving it as a country residence for the prime minister. That a prime minister could no longer be expected to own his own country seat is eloquent testimony to the passing of the old order.

As a result of the agricultural depression from the 1870s onwards, a minor industry sprang up restoring, enlarging and altering the whole flood of houses which came on to the market, many of them pre-Civil War manor houses, often reduced to the level of ruinous farmhouses. *Country Life* even ran a series entitled 'New Homes in Old Houses', and a large number of the examples in the series Country Homes and Gardens were also old houses which had been restored and modernised. Tipping, the magazine's architectural editor, was an avid enthusiast in doing up old houses: in 1894, he had purchased Mathern Palace, near Chepstow, the ruins of a medieval house, and later he embarked on an even more ambitious "restoration" not far away at Mounton House. The admired model for such restoration and enlargement, as far as the magazine was concerned, was a house called Great Tangley, Surrey. Work here had been carried out by Philip Webb for Wickham Flower, and *Country Life* was to return to it and its garden no less than three times before 1914. The magazine increasingly seemed to feature a roll-call of houses brought back from the grave: Lutyens' face-lift to Temple Dinsley, Detmar Blow's re-erection of the ruins of an Elizabethan manor house, Berwick St Leonard, or H. M. Fletcher's restoration of Cadhay.

These houses set the pattern for the future, indicating the more modest style of living that the house in the country now represented. Smaller in size than the great halls of the aristocracy, they were often rambling and organic in appearance and construction, and unassertive in their position in the landscape, unlike the grand architectural statements which dominated their surroundings. These houses necessitated a scaling down of living styles for their owners, and called for far fewer servants to run them. Many of these houses feature in stories of reclamation of the kind told in an article on G. F. Bodley's Water Eaton Manor, Oxford, in 1907, where three manor houses in proximity to each other were described as having been "used as farms and were decayed, if not ruinous … but since brought back to dignity and good condition". In the process of restoration, what was not actually old was made to look old as the new criteria for preserving buildings put out by such conservationist bodies as the Society for the Protection of Ancient Buildings took hold.

Country Life's sympathies may have lain with the great houses of the aristocracy, but its future rested with its expanding middle class readership who launched a building boom of small country houses which was to last until the outbreak of war in 1914. These people, with money from commerce, trade and professional life, wanted a house in the country with a garden and a few acres around it, enough to shoot and maybe including a home farm. They certainly did not want the responsibility of estate management. Trains, and then increasingly after 1900, the motor car, made the Home Counties of Kent, Sussex and Surrey easily accessible and that is where the majority of these new houses is to be found. The associated lifestyle was leisured and more informal, calling for a new arrangement of interior space in which family and visitors could encounter each other in the intimacy of meandering corridors, bay windows and nooks. This, the golden age of the weekend, required a house which could be "contracted" during the week but "expanded" from Friday evening to Monday morning to cope with the onrush of guests.

For two decades, *The Studio* (established in 1893) and *Country Life* magazines were to present to their readers a whole series of new and quite small houses, built by a younger generation of architects, although the latter's initial foray in this direction was chiefly confined to a prolonged public relations exercise for Edwin Lutyens. In December 1900, Gertrude Jekyll's home at Munstead Wood featured: "We do not hesitate to say that this modestly beautiful house, its wood and garden are clearly destined to become classical ..." Its gentle vernacular vocabulary of brick, timber and plaster stands out as a glaring exception amid the long procession of aggressive Victorian piles with their seas of bedding-out plants which dominated the magazine's early issues. Orchards, in Godalming, Surrey, followed the next year and then all the others by Lutyens, one by one as they were built. It is arguable how much of Lutyens' influence we can discern in defining the architectural taste of the magazine.

It was not until 1909, with "The Lesser Country Houses of Today", the brainchild of Lawrence Weaver, that a satisfactory shopwindow for new domestic architecture was found. In 1913, the magazine even ran a competition for the design of a small country house with six bedrooms. Weaver's series opened with Ernest Barnsley's Sapperton and went on to cover the work of a whole raft of architects, including Ernest Newton, Weir Schultz, Ernest Gimson, Detmar Blow and W.R. Lethaby. Many of these were made the subjects of supplements attached to the magazine and featured again in book form through Hudson's policy of recycling the magazine's contents. Never before in architectural history had so much visual information been available to those wishing to build a house.

(*Above*) *The mechanisation of the household developed after 1918 when servants were less obtainable. Here both maid and footman are still firmly in evidence.*

Those houses are now looked upon as the masterworks of a golden age of domestic building, reflecting an increased aesthetic awareness and a concern for the use of materials and the realities of modern living. The latter was evident in the multiplication of bathrooms, the use of electric light, central heating and the advent of the garage. Even the swimming pool makes an appearance. The style of these houses can be divided down the middle into two options, one was romantic and rambling, a kind of vernacular Tudorbethan, the other grander, with an eye turned towards Wren and the early Georgians, a style generally blanketed with the term Wrenaissance. Despite their modern amenities, both styles were backward-looking. Of the two retrospective fashions, sympathy tended to lie with the Tudorbethan, as one may gather from Lawrence Weaver's reaction to the onrush of neo-classical houses around 1910: "There is now a tendency among many of the younger men", he wrote, "to express a very earnest admiration for the Greek revivalists, but it is unlikely that the extreme severity of the interior decorations of that period will ever again become at all general …" His preference

(Below) Lutyens' dining room at The Deanery, Sonning, Berkshire, demonstrated a vernacular and relatively modest scale of living.

was for delicacy of texture and the colour of stone and brick, a worshipping of the ageing process and a passion for softening through the new naturalistic garden style of Jekyll.

This affection for a kind of "Olde English" style could also be seen in the interior decoration of these revamped or wholly new country homes. *Country Life*'s impact in this area was enormous, due to the manipulations of Hudson, Tipping and their photographer, Charles Latham, in rearranging rooms into suitably attractive "pictures". It would interesting to know who first hit upon the idea and, even more, how its results were received by the owners of the houses they photographed. They owe much to the lithographs in Joseph Nash's *The Mansions of England in the Olden Time* . Nash's reconstructions, which were originally published betwen 1839 and 1849 and were reprinted by *The Studio* in 1906, are almost interchangeable with Latham's photographs of "Tudor" and "Jacobean" interiors: there are the same sparsely furnished rooms with the solitary table, scattering of oak chairs and armour on the walls.

The earliest photograph of a country house interior in 1897 is of the library at Sledmere, an elegant Georgian interior awash with an explosion of Victorian bric-à-brac. There is certainly no hint of rearrangement here. The picture arrives on the pages almost by accident, for the photographer had been sent to cover the stud. Indeed, it is some time before the magazine's camera manages to get inside the great houses. Interiors appear in fits and starts and for almost a decade 'Country Homes and Gardens, Old and New' remained almost exclusively outside the buildings, circling their

(Left) Morris' own bedroom at Kelmscott Manor, Oxfordshire, which became a model of the Arts and Crafts style.

grounds for shots of their exteriors. Houghton Tower, Lancashire, in 1905, almost ten years on, is an early instance of an extensive photographic coverage of an interior. It is difficult not to sense the influence of Nash's prints in the presentation of these Jacobean rooms.

Under the aegis of Hudson and Tipping, the interior of a country house would be thinned out and redeployed to form a lyrical picture composed of old oak furniture, faded textiles and tapestries, sturdy pewter and brass utensils under the play of a golden light streaming in through mullioned windows. Such an arrangement was important in presenting an apparently authentic evocation of the past. The actual effect was, however, more akin to the type of interior favoured by the Arts and Crafts Movement, such as that designed by Philip Webb at Clouds, in which the rooms were light, airy and unencumbered, with simple panelling of unstained oak, relieved only by a touch of colour from William Morris fabrics.

These images led the middle classes to jettison their antimacassars and their extremely comfortable upholstered Victorian furniture, lavish draperies and wall-to-wall carpeting in favour of polished wooden floors with a scattering of rugs, uncomfortable oak furniture, whose only concession would be a squab cushion, and a sparse array of brass and pewter. Such an interior could be furnished with either genuine antiques or by a visit to Maples, the department store. In featuring antiques, *Country Life* was to have in its service two of the most influential figures in the history of the decorative arts in this country — Margaret Jourdain and Percy Macquoid. Both contributors were heavily involved with dealers and in advising collectors. From Hudson's point of view, here was another commercial opportunity. The magazine could pour out articles unravelling the evolution and history of antiques, and could exploit this interest to full financial advantage on the advertising pages with long streams of inviting pictures of what was available in the art and antiques trade.

These pioneering articles covered a tremendous variety of topics ranging as far as Anglo-Saxon drinking glasses to armour, from eighteenth-century furniture to the Hardwick Hunting tapestries. Whole series developed, like those by Lawrence Weaver on leadwork and Tipping on Renaissance woodwork. Even the furniture of particular houses came under scrutiny. These articles were important not only in terms of heightening people's awareness, but also because they encouraged serious reassessment of forgotten figures in the history of the arts in Britain. For the first time, the contents of the country houses of Britain were being examined with an analytical and informed eye. This was one approach which in spite of all its initial amateurishness, in fact paved the way to the highly-developed expertise evident in the magazine today.

(Opposite) Frederick Evans executed two great series of photographs of Norfolk and Suffolk churches for Country Life *which usually avoided illustrating things ecclesiastical.*

Cottages and Gardens

For those who could not afford to purchase an ancient mansion, restore a ruin or build a new country house, there was always the cottage. While *Country Life* worried about the lack of adequate housing for ordinary country people, it recommended at the same time the purchase of picturesque yeomen's houses and humble cottages as weekend retreats for the affluent middle class.

In March 1905, it dwelt on "the overwhelming advantage of [the cottage] being a thoroughly artistic and tasteful home, weathered and toned, and likely to resist the work of time". Artistic and tasteful, yes, but only after their advice of gutting anything remotely Victorian in date was heeded. Anything added was to be indistinguishable from the prevailing ethos of an "Olde English" interior style. The only thing that really did distinguish these converted properties was their inclusion of comforts unknown to their original occupants, but essential to those wishing to espouse the "simple life".

As early as 1902, the magazine actually billed 'The Cottage as Country House', extolling its virtues to the professional classes as answering the new "impulse to outdoor life", such as boating, bicycling, fishing, shooting and driving.

If the magazine was to fashion taste in domestic architecture and interiors, it was also to dictate change in the garden. In terms of longevity and importance, its coverage of gardens was especially significant and both set and reflected contemporary taste. Maintaining a garden had formerly involved a huge labour force, commanding which was the head gardener: this tradition was virtually obliterated in favour of the view that the garden was an expression of the owner's individualism. Creating a new garden from scratch demonstrated his sense of squirearchical responsibility: by laying out a garden, the landed gentleman indicated his connection with the past and his role as guardian of a monument which would be passed on to his heirs. Thus the role of the head gardener, that apogee of mid-Victorian life, came to an end.

As with architecture, the rediscovery of Tudor and Stuart garden styles emphasised the value of cottage gardens with their old-fashioned flowers. Places like Levens Hall, with its amazing topiary, represented the paradigm of what was believed to be the pre-industrial English garden. *Country Life* was fortunate in having Gertrude Jekyll, the high priestess of garden art, in its service and she wrote a column in the magazine for several decades.

Many of the most distinguished garden writers and designers of period also contributed to its pages: F. Inigo Thomas, Eden Philpotts, H. Inigo

(Opposite) Before 1914, the magazine was greatly concerned with rural housing and how it could be built cheaply. This was a specimen of an 'ideal cottage' at Merrow, Guildford, which could be erected at a reasonable price.

Triggs, William Robinson and Dean Hole. Avray Tipping, himself a garden designer, was also a potent influence on editorial attitudes to garden design: deeply committed to the principles enunciated by Miss Jekyll, he was also a personal friend of Harold Peto, the exponent of the Italianate style of garden design, a taste suited to newly rich aesthetes, suggesting the world of the Renaissance and the writings of Walter Pater and Jacob Burckhardt. Sir George Sitwell's garden at Renishaw was its harbinger, appearing in the magazine in 1900, and was a realisation of a long and eccentric obsession with the decayed beauty of the great formal gardens of Italy. But it was Peto's work which was recorded most often, Iford and Easton Lodge being the prime examples.

Gardens are perfect foils for photography and Latham's pictures of gardens are arguably greater than his ones of buildings and interiors. In 1909, Tipping described what gardens should not be:

> … The house emanated from the office with little regard to its site. The ground wound its gravel paths, extended its shrubberies, dotted its specimen plants, set its lobelia and calceolari circles, stars and crescents about the lawn without worrying itself where the house stood and what pictures it was going to make in connection with it.

Tipping condemned the High Victorian garden style with its accents on bedding-out, use of strident colour and disregard for the architectural unity of house and garden. There was, however, nothing particularly sensational in such an attack, for as long ago as 1883 William Robinson had published his famous attack, *The English Flower Garden*, with its advocation of old-fashioned English herbaceous plants, wild flowers and naturalistic planting.

Country Life appeared five years after the biggest horticultural row of the century, that caused by the publication of Reginald Blomfield's *The Formal Garden in England* in 1892. Although littered with inaccuracies, the book argued for the primacy of the architect in garden design, a view which Robinson regarded as anathema.

Nonetheless, Blomfield's book is a pioneering text, firmly locating true English gardening style in Tudor and Jacobean England, rather than in either the eighteenth century or the subsequent Victorian period. Blomfield pleaded for a formal structure in which clipped yew rooms, topiary, knot gardens, weathered outbuildings and sculpture linked house and garden with geometric unity. His vision was in tune with the demands of modern living: these seemingly ancient garden rooms made ideal venues for tennis, swimming, tea and garden parties.

However, gardens had one tremendous drawback: they could not, like the interiors, be deliberately manipulated other than through the selective view-

(Above) A fountain designed by Lutyens for Orchards, Surrey, one of the gardens he masterminded with Gertrude Jekyll.

(Opposite) Iford Manor, Wiltshire. Harold Peto's garden design in the new Italian style.

point of the camera. Exclusion was another possibility : the landscape style of the eighteenth century had to wait until the 1930s and Christopher Hussey's editorship to be rehabilitated within the magazine. *Country Life* was to provide its readers with a cornucopia of visual information for those wishing to add an "appropriate" garden to an old house or a new garden for a new house which was, of course, made to look old. Packwood, with its Sermon on the Mount (an array of stupendous clipped yew cones), and Montacute, with its supposedly Jacobean pond, were in fact not very old at all, but they figured high among the exemplars of the "Olde English" style.

These gardens had everything Blomfield thought essential: spaces divided geometrically by walls or clipped hedges planned in proportion to the house: raised terraces, gazebos, broad walks, alleys, flowerbeds and a symmetrical forecourt. To this framework was added a lavish planting of old-fashioned English herbaceous plants, presenting to the reader a resolution of rival gardening styles. Today we might view it as a combination of the use of a strong structure softened by abundant planting.

Some particular examples of the many gardens shown include Francis Inigo Thomas' work at Rotherfield Hall, where he created a garden he believed was in keeping with the sentiments of its original designers, and which had the appearance of having grown naturally over the centuries. The works of Thomas' follower, Blomfield, also featured in the magazine: Knowlton Court, Godington and Apethorpe Hall.

Most important of all was the large amount of space given to the work of Edwin Lutyens and Gertrude Jekyll, which established the reconciliation of styles through an architectural inventiveness combined with mature plantsmanship, an approach which determined the direction of British gardening for the rest of the century. Their landmark was Orchards, Surrey, a vernacular sandstone house, whose lines were projected outwards along routes and vistas. The garden's architecture was a multiplication of the forms and shapes of the house itself, making the house seem larger. The garden structure was then broken down by Jekyll's planting with its use of calculated sprawl and deployment of climbers on walls and pergolas.

(Above) A decorative heading from 1898.

(Opposite) A bowler-hatted gardener hand-clipping the massive Victorian topiary garden at Elvaston Castle, Derbyshire.

THE ENGLISH ARCADIA

(Left) The Wyck, Hitchin, Hertfordshire, the
new ideal of a country house for the readers of
Country Life. Such rambling houses exuded
the aura of security and comfortable
domesticity sought by the predominantly
urban-based middle classes.

The greatest examplar of garden style for the magazine was Great Tangley: around its restored half-timbered Elizabethan manor house stretched a garden which represented the culmination of the ideals of the Arts and Crafts Movement, characterised by bridges and walks of sturdy oak timbers protected by tiled roofs, rustic pergolas, topiary in yew and box, neatly clipped hedges defining spaces, and beyond, a plantsman's paradise of meandering walkways.

Tipping might have been describing such a garden plan in his address to the Royal Horticultural Society in 1928: "Let there be formality about the house to carry on the geometric lines and enclosed feeling of architecture, but let us step shortly from that into the wood and wild garden."

The Arts and Crafts garden made use of local materials and plants, favoured the weathered patina of stone or brick (the outdoor equivalent of the antiques within), and articulated garden space by means of hedges, trellis, walls and pergolas, delighting the eye with a profusion of soft colour.

These were the gardens which received praise and coverage by *Country Life*, and they were of a style which was essentially middle class with particular appeal for the new professional classes who were buying homes in the country in increasing numbers. Other styles spread like a temporary rash through Edwardian gardens, such as the craze for things Japanese, but even though Lawrence Weaver featured a garden in that style at Powerscourt, Ireland, in 1915, his intention was mainly to censure it:

> The importation of exotic motifs into garden design in England is dangerous not only because they are rarely understood, but because there are few sites where they can take their place at all naturally. The disposition of a few typical ornaments, of a bronze stork here and a stone lantern there, does not make a Japanese garden.

By the end of 1914, *Country Life* had established an immutable repertory of values and visual models which were to remain at the core of the magazine's editorial vision for the next eighty years.

But a sinister cloud had appeared on the political horizon, the consequences of which were to challenge the magazine's vision forever. The declaration of war had interrupted the peace of Arcadia.

Arcadia at War

Country Life had ignored the Boer War, but its reaction to the First World War was to be quite different. The decision to pledge the magazine's resources to the war effort must have been taken by Edward Hudson by 15th August 1914 (war had been declared on 4th August), when that issue's editorial called on the upper classes "to live sparingly". The magazine was filled with a miscellany of articles related to the future war effort, such as the importance of wild fruits in the hedgerows as a source of food, the role of rifle clubs in training, how horses could be gathered together from their farming and hunting roles for shipment to the front and an article on "How to increase the Food Supply".

The war was never to leave the pages of *Country Life* for its duration. The pre-war stage-managed tableau of rural life vanished, as did the lyrical pictures of seasonal beauty. The frontispiece portraits suddenly ceased to have a Ruritanian tinge to them, and aristocratic ladies were now included on account of their war work. The portraits even gave way to images of the war leaders themselves. But articles on country homes and gardens survived in much the same way they had done before the war. They provided a balance for the grim diet of the realities of war, which did not shirk from featuring vividly-illustrated eye-witness accounts of the fate of men and horses. No words were spared in condemning the barbarity of the Huns, as photographs listed cathedrals, towns and farmsteads blasted by their bombs.

The England the troops were fighting for was one propagated by the magazine, the country mythologised by poets like E. V. Lucas: "O England, country of my heart's desire, land of the hedgerow and the village spire." The war was cast as a battle against the rapacious Germans, who threatened English woods, villages, streams and the nation's womanhood. Although only 20% of the population lived in the countryside, the nation's patriotism drew inspiration from images drawn from the country's rural past as it had been represented in the decades preceeding 1914. As the war progressed, the pre-war cult of the countryside, epitomised by *Country Life*, intensified. Manor houses, medieval churches, tithe barns and thatched cottages all became symbols of English life which must remain eternal. The longer the war lasted, the more important these images of rural tranquillity were to become. The poet Rupert Brooke's early death and his poem "The Old Vicarage, Grantchester" created a steadfast image of Englishness which was to hold a nation together.

Each editorial page bore the exhortation "to our readers to send their copies of recent issues of COUNTRY LIFE to the TROOPS AT THE FRONT". All that was needed was to take them, unwrapped, to the nearest

(Opposite) The frontispiece of the magazine on 1st January 1916 showing the Duchess of Westminster in her nurses' uniform.

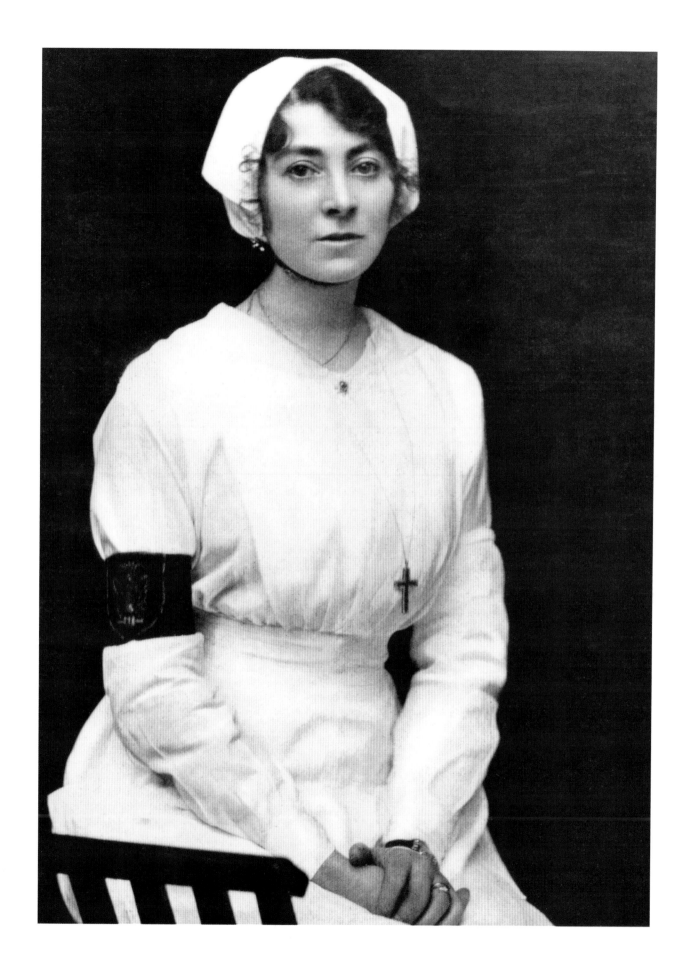

(Above) Women road-menders on a Hertfordshire highway, an image which highlights the changing role of women in society.

post office and they would be sent on. *Country Life* thus found its way into the muddiest of the trenches in the battle zone, proving hugely popular reading matter for the officer class. One young subaltern wrote home to his father: "I'm devilish glad to get *COUNTRY LIFE* and sick when it sometimes gets delayed. The only trouble is that it wears out with the rough handling we all give it."

One senses the death knell of a civilisation during these fateful years. By 1918, it was clear that the way of life for the upper classes pre-1914 could never return. Already by 22nd August 1914, Devonshire House, the great London palace of the Dukes of Devonshire, had become the temporary headquarters of the Red Cross. The magazine's photographs remain a precious record of a doomed architectural ensemble. "The owners of great mansions are reminding us, by their noble offers, of the national utilities of houses of a scale and size adequate to exigencies of times of war." There followed practical advice as to how a country house could be turned into a hospital — how rooms could be emptied, what was needed in the way of beds, linen and toilets. "It is a noble thing to offer one's entire house and to hand it over for the use of the sick and suffering." The closure of the great London houses and the transformation of country houses into hospitals and convalescent homes were seen as merely temporary measures. But as the

THE ENGLISH ARCADIA

war ground on, it was clear that something irreversible had occurred. The first great exodus of men to the war consisted of those who volunteered in response to the huge surge of patriotism which swept the country at its outbreak. In July 1915 *Country Life* recorded:

> When war broke out Lord Derby set himself to raise recruits, not by the thousand, but by the tens of thousands … his territorial influence spreads wide throughout the county, but it is strongest in the Liverpool area, and there he put in his most assiduous work. Battalion after battalion was raised …

What was true of a great Lancashire magnate was equally so of a Nottinghamshire landowner. The Duke of Portland declared at a recruiting meeting that he would have "felt nothing less than a despicable wretch had not his son and every other member of the family bearing the name Bentinck come forward at the present moment". All work at the vast mansion house of Welbeck Abbey came to a standstill in order to release hundreds of estate workers for the war. The Duchess took up hospital work and the great ballroom and indoor tennis court were soon transformed into wards. The Duke, following the example set by the king, George V, locked the Abbey's wine cellars for the duration of the war.

But this was not quite the whole story. In September 1914, *Country Life*

(Above) 'Modes and Moods'. The magazine's fashion column included items suitable to wear for labouring on the land.

(Left) Women workers in a munitions factory in 1918, reflecting not only a change in the status of women but also the relaxation of union rules.

To Die with Honour

LIEUT. G. LEIGH PEMBERTON

MAJOR AUBREY BUCKINGHAM

(Above and Opposite) County by county, Country Life *recorded the toll taken of the upper classes by the war.*

published a defensive explanation of the "apparent apathy of the rural population to the call to arms" by J. L. Green: "In the first place, it was highly important that the harvest should be garnered: and, in the second place, news filters into the rural mind slowly." As a result, a small army of recruiters was sent into the villages to spread "a knowledge of German perfidy, German aggression and German malice". What *Country Life* did not record was that many landowners threatened their employees with redundancy unless they volunteered. By Christmas 1914, the magazine could record:

> the mutter of rifle shooting and the roar of heavy guns have become far more familiar than the whistle of the steam plough and the din of the threshing-machine ... Quiet, secluded lanes daily witness the march of infantry and are churned into mud by the heavy artillery.

The war, which many believed would be over by Christmas, was to last over four long years. In January 1915, *Country Life* posed five questions to its upper class readers:

1. Have you a Butler, Groom, Chauffeur, Gardener, or Gamekeeper serving you who, at this moment should be serving your King and Country?
2. Have you a man serving at your table who should be serving a gun?
3. Have you a man digging your garden who should be digging trenches?
4. Have you a man driving your car who should be driving a transport wagon?
5. Have you a man preserving your game who should be helping to preserve your Country?

A great responsibility rests on you. Will you sacrifice your personal convenience for your Country's need? Ask your men to enlist TO-DAY.

The accounts of Lord Derby's and the Duke of Portland's recruiting drives featured in a series of articles which began on 10th July 1915 covering each county and entitled 'What the Country Gentleman has done for the War'. In every issue, the uniformed faces of those serving, wounded or fallen on the field of battle, stare out hauntingly at the reader. The opening article was on Dorset and Wiltshire, with a roll call of ancient county families: Methuens, Herberts, Thynnes and Wyndhams. By the close of 1914, six peers, sixteen baronets, ninety-five sons of peers and eighty-two sons of baronets had been killed. The great landed aristocratic and gentry families faced their losses with stoicism and a deep commitment to the idea of sacrifice. Funeral hatchments were hung above the door of manor houses, the flag bearing the family arms fluttered at half-mast and the sword of the vanquished was solemnly laid on the steps of the altar of the parish church. *Country Life* soon had articles and advertisements on war memorials. This war was unlike any other that had preceeded it. Gentlemen laid down their lives in what it became quickly apparent was a far from gentlemanly way — they were mown down amidst the mud and barbed wire of the trenches of Flanders.

Since estate owners often took their workers with them when they enlisted, entire village communities were devastated in the resulting onslaught. In September 1915, *Country Life* recorded the toll taken of some in Berkshire: Basildon sent forty-nine; Ilsey forty out of five hundred; Leckhampstead thirty-four out of two hundred and fifty and Buckland seventy-nine out of four hundred and ninety-three. By January 1915, 15% of all farm labourers in England and Wales had joined up or been requisitioned for government work. So many were taken that those who could plough had to be released to ensure food production. What this sudden dislocation of the status quo of rural working patterns averted by default, however, was the clash of landowner and agricultural worker which had been edging towards crisis just before 1914. Now landlord, tenant and worker found themselves side by side in the trenches, dissolving, *Country Life* recorded in December 1915:

> the barbed wire entanglements of class distinctions of which society is ordinarily composed ... Before the war these divisions had a tendency to expand. To-day we meet a situation in which the consciousness of dignity in one is tempered and mitigated, and the spirit of the other raised and confirmed. The nobleman in his castle and the plain man in his cottage; the sportsman who hunted the countryside, and the artisan whose sport was confined within the four corners of a football field, heard the 'Fall in' sounded on trumpet and bugle, and they are now joined together in one great army fighting 'to play the game', not for themselves alone, but King and country.

Country Life also recorded the abilities of the officer class to recreate on the front the sporting life they knew at home — that is, until 1915, when the French banned hunting and shooting. In December 1914, an officer in the Royal Field Artillery sent the magazine a sketch of his ideal Christmas leave. It showed a huntsman, hounds at his horse's feet, blowing his horn. But at home in England, the hunt was on its way to becoming a thing of the past. As shortages bit ever deeper, it was increasingly difficult to justify feeding horses and hounds for sport. Shooting also contracted. By 1st May

FOR KING AND COUNTRY

CAPTAIN RUPERT MURRAY

CAPTAIN FANE MURRAY

(Above and Opposite) These photographs featured in an article entitled 'What Kent has done for the War'.

1915, *Country Life* was reporting that on many estates, where vast numbers of pheasants were usually raised, "no eggs at all are being set this year". In 1917, in order to protect the crops, the government allowed tenant-farmers to shoot those pheasants intruding onto their land, a decision bemoaned by two contributors to the magazine. But the attempts by some estate owners to pretend nothing had changed were to prove delusory.

Just as officers tried to pursue country sports inches away from potential death, so their interest in nature remained undiminished. Another officer wrote about an owl, *Athene noctua*, which he remembered hearing the previous year in a Kentish orchard. Ignoring the Germans, during the nesting season of 1915 he climbed up a tree in what was left of the devastated wood and succeeded in photographing the bird's nest: "And yet the wood is shelled by the enemy every day, several dead cows are rotting in the track through it, and many of the trees are smashed by the explosions ..." In August 1915, Arnold Bennett reported to the magazine's readers an even more extraordinary phenomenon only five miles from the German trenches: "the whole of the earth seems to be cultivated and to be yielding bounteously". *Country Life's* explanation for this "strange and prodigal abundance" was that the

> chemical fertilisers and munitions come largely from the same source ... the explosives contain large quantities of nitric acid or nitrates and potash. The unburnt part of these explosives accounts for the extraordinary plant growth ... By a grim irony, the fertilisers which were extracted from German agriculture to be used in killing the French have had the effect of fertilising the fair fields of France.

While the war was an engineer of social change for men, it was even more so for women. Daughters of manor house owners became nurses, canteen and factory workers, thrown together with women who, before 1914, would have been their servants. The old bounds of etiquette collapsed as the ritual of chaperonage broke down. The shift of attitudes was swift. In the month of the outbreak of war, *Country Life* exhorted women "to set to work as speedily as may be arranging and making comforts and garments for the brave men fighting for the honour and glory of their country". Under a year later, in May 1915, Lady Londonderry used the magazine to launch what became the Women's Legion. This was divided into four sections, of which one was for agriculture. It was not to prove a success and in the end the Board of Agriculture, set up to increase food production, was to restrict its activities to fruit bottling and horticulture. But Lady Londonderry's Legion was not the only women's organisation involved in agriculture. There were others, above all the Women's Land Army. *Country Life* recorded the work

(Opposite) Northborough Manor. All through the war the country house continued to be presented as an unchanging bastion.

of women on the land in a series of articles begun in June 1916 accompanied by pictures which capture astonishing scenes, such as women engaged in mending country roads. In spite of this, the magazine felt that British women fell short when compared with their Belgian and French counterparts who laboured in the fields almost up to the line of battle. In September 1915, these were held up as examples for the landowners of Britain to emulate "where every man of military age is absent from the fields and the land is cropped right up to the firing line".

For the women who remained at home on the estates, their energies went into food production. There was a campaign of self-denial, launched in August 1915, in which aristocratic ladies pledged themselves to cut their expenditure on imported goods, to curtail all luxuries, to simplify their dress, to cut back on food and entertaining and to refuse to employ as a servant any man who was elegible for military service.

The war changed the face of the countryside. Three thousand acres of grassland were ploughed up; a thousand acres were requisitioned for army and prison camps; and the woodlands were devastated for timber. The horse all but vanished from the rural scene. This was the saddest conesquence of all, for the army not only took horses from the farms but also those from the stables of manor houses. *Country Life* records the taking of the hunting horses, packed into trains and despatched to the scene of the action. "How

(Above) Horses carry ammunition through the mud of Flanders.

76

many will ever again hear the sound of the horn", it plaintively asked. The magazine and the countryside in general concentrated on one priority: increasing the supply of food. By the close of the war, farmers were to produce enough to feed the population for one hundred and fifty-five days of the year as compared with the hundred and twenty-five at the war's beginning. But the necessity to start this process dawned slowly. The government was faced with the reluctance of farmers to plough up their pastorage. Only as overseas supplies were cut off, owing to the activities of the German U-boats, did shortages set in of cereals, sugar, fertilisers and animal feed. Prices started to rocket. Farmers, of course, made huge profits. *Country Life* records one who made £20,000 from potatoes. As a consequence, price controls were introduced by the close of 1916.

The government, in the guise of the Milner Committee, took measures to increase home production. Their recommendation was to offer subsidies to the farmers, but that idea was rejected with the result that production actually lessened in 1916-1917, after which the government opted not only for a minimum wage for farm workers but also a guaranteed price for wheat and oats for a period of six years. All of this was enshrined in the Corn Production Act of 1917. Two and half million acres of land in England and

(Below) An officers' mess.

THE ENGLISH ARCADIA

Wales were ploughed up as a result. There were, however, two other developments to which much magazine space was devoted: land reclamation and agricultural mechanisation. The former represented a reversal of the previous four decades, so that by 1918, pastorage levels had fallen back to where they had been in 1890. The war also forced farmers to use the tractor. *Country Life* referred to agricultural machinery as the "ammunition of the land army". The long series of articles dedicated to 'Machinery Notes for Modern Farmers' signalled the future parallel between farming and factory production, making use of all forms of mechanical contrivance and — a necessity accelerated by the loss of horses — abundant recourse to chemical fertilisers. Photographs of agricultural yields grown with or without the application of sulphate of ammonia made the comparison clear. In the last year of the war, *Country Life* applauded the productivity of the farmers:

> it represents the energy and resolution of the British farmers, who, when confronted with the menace that the food supplies would be cut off by submarine warfare, ploughed and harrowed, weeded and sowed until they had more ground under the plough than has ever been before in the records of British husbandry.

In every sphere, the old way of life was disintegrating. The Corn Production Act represented an unprecedented interference with private property rights, prohibiting increases in farm rentals and enforcing the cultivation of land. The cost of living rose by 49% and the price for farm products by a factor of almost 59%. Those were not the only things to bite deeply into the ability of the landed classes to maintain their old way of life. Added to them were the anxiety and grief of personal loss, as well as a declining income, a lack of servants and rationing. Increased running costs of the country houses, soaring taxation, rising interest rates and death duties, hastened the pace of change. The return on land, too, was amounting to a mere 2% of its capital value. *Country Life* wrote:

> Our contention ... is that the regulation forbidding the increase of rents ... is discouraging the flow of landlords' capital into agriculture ... if a man has no sport in a country, no profit and no nothing, except indeed it be taxation, of which there is more than enough, he has more inducement to sell his land than to improve it.

By 1917, the number of sales of estates began to rise and by the close of the following year, in the immediate hiatus brought by the end of the war,

(Above) The terrace of Lord Lee of Fareham's house, Chequers, Great Missenden, Buckinghamshire, with troops convalescing.

an article entitled 'Land and the Estate Market' spelt out the new reality: "The countryside is changing from month to month. Estates are in the process of disruption." There then followed a roll call of recent sales or ones in the offing including 3,000 acres of Lord Desborough's Panshanger estate, over 2,000 acres of the Oakley estate near Bedford, over 7,000 acres of the Alton estate in Staffordshire and some 238,000 acres of the Sutherland estates. These sales as often as not included the mansion house itself.

Of the landowning classes, it was the gentry who were most affected. The large aristocratic estates had far greater room for manoeuvre. Between 1918 and 1922, a quarter of the land surface of Britain changed hands. It marked in one sense a social revolution, finally dissolving the old ties which had bound country communities together for centuries. This dissolution was brought on not only by the economic necessity to meet taxes and retrench but also through the volte-face in the social perception of land as an unproductive encumbrance. Although taxation and a falling income may have forced many to sell up, several sales were a recognition of an irreversible shift: that land no longer brought social prestige and that, instead, political power and cash were now better placed in the City. Thanks to the need for home grown food, agriculture was undergoing a boom and it was therefore the ideal time to sell land. The losers were to be the tenant farmers who, after the brief post-war period of prosperity, were saddled with mortgages for the farms which they purchased and which they found difficult to meet. By 1922, the agricultural slump had returned with a vengeance.

On the whole, this huge revolution in ownership passed unnoticed. Although the advertisements in *Country Life* made it clear that enormous change was happening, the myth of the historical continuity of England was reinforced rather than diminished by the war. "She was Merrie England five hundred years ago and more", ran an editorial in January 1916, "and her sons and daughters have a serene confidence that she will be Merrie England again when this war is over."

So, the pictures of men in the trenches and women in factories or on the land, which made such startling features in *Country Life* during these years, became veiled by the more stabilising vision of country houses and gardens. At the Annual General Meeting of George Newnes Ltd held at the Savoy in 1918, the assembled shareholders heard that:

> *Country Life* has no competitor. It stands alone amongst illustrated publications as the paper which best portrays the characteristics of one of the chief and most important phases of our national life. The inquiry is often made whether *Country Life* is not coming to the end of the beautiful houses which are illustrated each week, but there is still, I am glad to say, an ample supply. *Country Life* has not yet exhausted the architectural treasures of this wonderful country.

Only those in the know realised that the sudden obsession with houses in Shropshire related to the fact that travel was difficult and that Avray Tipping lived not far away near Chepstow.

Taste inevitably moved on even during the war years. The Georgian revival of the post-war era began with a major reappraisal of the architecture of the age of Robert Adam. A long series of articles on London clubs, Whites for example, town houses, like those in Portland Place, and on cities such as Bath, appeared. This reappraisal moves the model of acceptable architecture on in date from the Tudor exempla of earlier issues.

Although Lawrence Weaver was under war service in 1916, the series on smaller country houses and other contemporary buildings continued, focusing in the main on the comforts of neo-Georgian housing of the type found in Hampstead Garden suburb.

The fashionable architectural style epitomised by Gertrude Jekyll's house at Munstead Wood — a kind of new Tudor, but managing to look centuries old at the same time — was spreading rapidly, becoming bastardised as it

was seized upon by provincial architects and builders for the burgeoning middle classes. The results were often picturesque, mellow, attractive and extremely comfortable, but it is undeniable that *Country Life* was recording the style which was to be parodied as "Stockbroker Tudor" by Osbert Lancaster in his book *Homes Sweet Homes* in 1939. The magazine began to show signs of unease at this architectural trend and Lawrence Weaver attacked this mock cottage architecture in the year before he left the magazine: "The Thatched Cottage would look more reasonable as a farmhouse in a country district than it does in the rather sophisticated rural area of this outer suburb of London."

But *Country Life* was merely reaping the seeds of what it had sown. Town architecture, Weaver explained, required an architectural unity expressed in gracious squares and terraces. But that had gone. In its place was a burgeoning suburbia of neo-Georgian and mock Tudor.

In the middle of the war, *Country Life* produced its thousandth issue and reiterated its credo: "One Cause, One Empire ... no people under the sun prize country life more than the British, and that the journal which more than any other reflects this tendency is by the fact national and imperial."

No evidence supports this claim in an issue which was unquestioning and celebratory in tone. As far as country houses were concerned, the magazine had the status already of being "an historical document".

In the realm of gardening, it had charted "an awakening to the conventionalism and formality of the Victorian garden and a renewed appreciation of the natural grace, harmonious colour and general freedom". For nature lovers "natural history was not only illustrated, it was transacted on our pages". The same was true of sport, for it recorded "the games and pastimes of the day as they were actually played".

As for the small house, some three hundred articles had presented the reader with the fruits of a renaissance in domestic architecture inaugurated by George Devey, Philip Webb, Norman Shaw and Eden Nesfield: "Never was domestic architecture more free, more subtle, more ready to accept new ideas and to hear fresh voices. The Battle of the Styles ... has given place to a tolerance born not of indifference but of understanding." There was as yet no hint of the architectural angst which was to come with the arrival of the Modernist Movement.

This upbeat atmosphere returned to the full at the close of 1918. The issue of 7th December captures the new mood exactly, with articles on 'The Future of Fox Hunting', 'Shooting after the War', 'The Re-birth of Racing' and 'The Revival of Cricket'.

In reality, however, nothing was ever to be quite the same again.

(Left) Hampstead Garden Suburb, London, part of the magazine's coverage of new domestic architecture.

REACTION
1918–1945

Keeping the Faith

When the First World War ended, most of the team which had created *Country Life* were still there. Edward Hudson and Avray Tipping, who died in 1936 and 1929 respectively, exerted a powerful influence on the magazine right up to the outbreak of the Second World War. The magazine continued to grow in size, the largest single issue during the inter-war years running to as many as three hundred pages. Special annual numbers, dedicated to subjects such as motoring, began to be issued and colour illustrations started to appear in the 1920s, with the first colour cover in 1931.

Hudson and Tipping were fortunate in selecting successors to run the magazine who adhered to the tradition they had established, one which was thus continued until 1970. In the case of photography, A. E. Henson (1885-1972) was Charles Latham's successor, covering country houses from 1917 to 1957. An obituary in the magazine recorded Henson as having "a determination in his work amounting to at times a thrust to the ruthless … He was of medium height, with a neat moustache and wax-like pallor …" A slow, crusty, difficult man, he stuck to the Latham formula of "arranged" illustrative fiction. Domestics were dragooned to move the furniture around or out of sight. Sometimes a piece of furniture which took his fancy would appear again and again in different shots. Blinds had to be drawn down and the ensuing light effects strictly controlled. In the garden, the lawns had to be mowed in a particular direction. Henson took no chances and developed his photographs on site. Henson was indeed a fine photographer, but his work lacks the lyrical magic of his predecessor. It represents a gradual shift in the magazine from a romantic to a scientific approach to photography, the latter taken up by his successor Alex Starkey.

Architectural feature articles remained at the heart of the magazine. Arthur Oswald joined *Country Life* in 1928, and was to write for it until his retirement in 1969. A shy and retiring academic, his articles reflect the increasing level of scholarship being applied to journalism about architecture but, it cannot be denied, his writing was worthy rather than inspired. His contribution to the magazine was second only to that brought by Christopher Hussey (1899-1970), whose influence was similar to Hudson's. He was to be associated with *Country Life* for sixty years. John Cornforth, a subsequent architectural editor and a friend of Hussey, wrote of him: "It is a story that explains a great deal about *Country Life*, its stability and success … and the values that it continues to stand for …" Hussey in his view was "a practical philosopher, an intellectual Whig".

Hussey, as we shall see, was a crucial figure in the debate about modernism which unfolded on its pages during the 1920s and 1930s, and

(Previous page) Penns in the Rocks, Sussex, Lord Gerald Wellesley, later Duke of Wellington, lived here in the 1920s.

(Right) Alnwick Castle, Northumberland. Economy forced its owner to close it in 1922.

(Above) Christopher Hussey was to be the dominant influence on the magazine right up to the 1960s. Although a pioneering architectural historian, he was deeply out of kilter with the modern age.

against which he was eventually to be a strong advocate. It is arguable that his viewpoint, expressed for the first time in the magazine's history, was responsible for its gradual aesthetic atrophy. Until Hussey, *Country Life* had supported and featured the work of all the up-and-coming architects. This was to change as the new styles of the twentieth century were eventually viewed by Hussey despite his initial interest and even enthusiasm, as inimical to the very ideals of Englishness propagated by the magazine.

Christopher Hussey, nephew and heir of the owner of Scotney Castle in Kent, came from the old landed classes and was educated in the appropriate manner at first Eton and then Oxford. Early on, he had been selected by Avray Tipping, who knew his parents, as his successor. From childhood, Hussey was artistically inclined, with a keen interest in architecture, drawing and writing. He shared with Tipping a passion for theatre and amateur theatricals and it was Hussey who was to cover the Diaghilev ballet for *Country Life*. When still at Oxford, he had written the occasional article for the magazine and joined its staff in 1921. He was its editor from 1933 to 1940, and architectural advisor until 1964, but his attitudes dominated the magazine right until his death in 1970. There is no doubting his contribution to architectural scholarship, a fact readily acknowledged by contemporary historians: one need only recall that Sir John Summerson was, for a brief period in the 1930s, on the staff and that Mark Girouard began his career under Hussey's aegis, to appreciate the enormous legacy he left in opening up the study of British domestic architecture. This legacy was not only represented by his own pieces in the magazine but also through the separate volumes published by *Country Life* covering country houses period by period. It was a formidable achievement in an era when country house archives were barely accessible and certainly were not even catalogued. He was a superb stylist which makes his articles a delight to read today.

In one sense, Hussey's influence was directly beneficial to *Country Life* in that he represented all that it held dear: his patriotic nature, revealed by his first book, *The Fairy Land of England*, reveals his turn-of-the-century vision of England as a land whose heart was the countryside, with rolling hills and peaceful lowlands punctuated by villages clustering round the church and manor house. When he eventually came into the Scotney estate, Cornforth writes, he "combined his intellectual life with that of being a country squire". Whether acting the farmer striding across a field or bellowing a hymn in church on Sundays he appeared to be living out the role of a paternalistic landowner who had adapted to the democratic age. But in a deeply revealing letter to his wife, Hussey actually descibed what Scotney meant to him: a "background, retreat, never-never land".

This retreat from reality, always nascent in *Country Life*, came to the fore under Hussey's editorship, for it is difficult to believe that he had much sympathy for the changes brought by the age in which he lived. Increasingly, *Country Life* became the magazine which reflected an era and society which had lost its energy. This drift into escapism took place during a period when the countryside changed with terrifying rapidity. It became accessible as never before, as cars flooded onto the roads until, by 1939, they numbered about 2.5 million. Villages and towns were closely linked for the first time by regular bus services. The development of public and privately-owned transport signalled the urbanisation of village life with the arrival of piped water and electricity. Deliveries, the doctor's visit and the school bus all became the norm, spelling the demise of the old village trades, the blacksmith, the wheelwright and the saddler. Bureaucracy began to impinge on everyone's life: in place of the landowners came, by way of various Local Government Acts, Urban and Rural District Councils to cope with planning applications, the building of council houses for farmworkers, the collection of rents and the execution of a whole raft of new legislation

(Below) Scotney Castle, Lamberhurst, Kent, which Christopher Hussey inherited.

affecting country life. Increasingly, the remaining traditions of feudal land-ownership disappeared and tensions between the countryside's residential and farming populations increased. The manor house, minus its acres, was purchased by the new rich, often only for use at weekends. The cottages and houses in the village were acquired and prettified by commuters, week-enders or the retired. While these changes of ownership resulted in a polarity between the new arrivals and the farmers, one which still exists today, it could only increase *Country Life*'s readership.

After 1918, the spread of the country life ethic espoused by the magazine spread well beyond the middle classes: it was embraced by the Conservative Prime Minister, Stanley Baldwin, who deliberately cultivated the rural-based image of Britain put forward by a whole series of authors, led by the historian G. M. Trevelyan, whose writings are an elegy to a vanished rural nation destroyed by the Industrial Revolution. Commercialism and indus-trialism, along with the businessman, were derided features of modern life, and "true spiritual" and human values were seen to be symbolised by the unfolding rituals of the agricultural year, with the honest yeoman praised as the model everyman.

All of this only added to the continuing and phenomenal success of *Country Life*. This was reflected in the large book publishing programme which continued until the 1960s. This had started between 1906 and 1909 with Charles Latham's three volumes of photographs entitled *In English Homes*. Tipping published his nine volumes of *English Homes* between 1920 and 1937. By the 1930s, Country Life Books had expanded to cover a whole range of subjects, from architecture, decorative arts, garden design, sport, natural history, and children's books — a catalogue of almost two hundred and fifty titles. Some were very practical, like *Lighting the Home*, the first scientific work on domestic lighting; Sir Lawrence Weaver's books *Cottages: Their Planning, Design and Materials* and *Gardens for Small Country Houses*, written with Gertrude Jekyll, went to several editions. The list contains some surprises: Bill Brandt's *A Night in London* and Katherine Hale's *Orlando, the Marmalade Cat*. Although this imprint vanished when *Country Life* was taken over by IPC Magazines in 1976, its book publishing wing had generated a massive amount of material for its readers.

In an editorial for 7th January 1922, entitled 'The Spirit of "Country Life"', it was concluded that the magazine "might probably be defined as teaching what to admire". The greatest examples of this, the editorial cites, were provided by "the beautiful old houses in England". The fact that they were beautiful cannot be denied, but unlike the era prior to 1914, such houses and the way of life they embodied were to become more remote than ever.

(Previous page) The village of Finchinfield, Essex, in the first decade of this century, and the winner of many best-kept village prizes.

(Opposite) A typical page of property advertisements for the 1920s.

The Servants Depart

The euphoria of winning the war did not last long, and was replaced by a period of fear and conflict which dominated the six years before Stanley Baldwin became Prime Minister in 1924. The editorials of *Country Life* are one long chronicle of social strife, both actual and potential, as cheap labour finally vanished and strike followed strike. "Revolution is in the air", ran one editorial in July 1920, "and the fiery spirits who lead it are particularly anxious that this country should be involved." Servants wages doubled, and there was no lessening of the burden of taxation on the middle classes. "A man for the garden and a maid for the house is surely a minimum of service ..." piped a December issue, with the melodramatic assertion that "Civilisation itself is threatened."

All the upper classes were affected by these social upheavals. For the seriously rich, they meant a contraction of lifestyle, but for vast tracks of the middle classes, the automatic provision of domestic and other "service", previously taken for granted, vanished. This, in turn, triggered what can only be described as a bitterness and a resentment against working class prosperity, seemingly achieved at the expense of the middle classes. The miners' strike of 1921 was viewed as the work of "Lenin and his fellow-workers ... In especial their activities are directed towards Great Britain because they look upon this country as the great European capital of Capitalism." The astonishing rise of the Labour Party to power (Ramsay MacDonald became its first Prime Minister in 1924) was looked upon with horror. This was a political party based on hand-outs to the unemployed: "Strong men and strong nations are not produced by coddling, but by hardship", thundered the magazine.

Nowhere is the magazine's conservative political and social stance more forcefully stated than in an editorial in September 1922, entitled "The Oppression of the Middle Classes":

> ... the trend of political statesmanship in this country is to encourage the least efficient section of the population to have children and to discourage the intelligent middle class ... [who] are the most oppressed, the most hardly-tried of all sections of the population.

No words of condemnation were adequate enough for those who sponged on the state — "the degrading effect of pampering those who live in idleness" — or for the short-lived premiership of Ramsay MacDonald. Sidney and Beatrice Webb were violently attacked for their advocacy of a 100% tax on landlords. These attacks were based on real political possibilities: throughout 1924, there hung the pall of the nationalisation of land.

(Opposite) Glyndebourne, Sussex, opened in 1938, giving the country house a new lease of life as an opera house.

TOUR THE COUNTRY—IN A BEAN

GET into touch with the countryside this year—but first get into touch with the Bean Car. No other car in the Bean class will give you as much pleasure on the road. Bean efficiency—economy—safety—and simplicity are all reasons why the Bean car excels.

The equipment includes everything that you can desire. And every Bean car is fitted with Four-wheel brakes (Perrot-Servo type), Four-speed gear box, right hand control. Exceptionally roomy four-door body with front seats and all controls adjustable, spare wheel and tyre, electric lighting set, etc. Dunlop tyres are standard. For illustrated catalogue please write to manufacturer.

A. HARPER, SONS & BEAN, LTD.

Allied with Hadfields Ltd., Sheffield.

HEAD OFFICE AND WORKS - - DUDLEY, WORCESTERSHIRE.
Telephone : 2469 Dudley. Telegrams : " Waddams," Dudley
LONDON SHOWROOMS - 11a REGENT STREET, S.W.1
'Phone : Gerrard 7672-3. Wires : " Salobean," Piccy, London.
COMMERCIAL VEHICLE DEPT. - NORTH ROAD, CALEDONIAN ROAD, N.7
'Phone : North 3609 (4 lines). Wires : " Servibean," Holway, London.
MANCHESTER DISTRIBUTING DEPOT - WOOD STREET (off DEANSGATE)
'Phone : Central 1016. Wires : " Trabeapo," Manchester.

BEAN CARS
Our 1926 Centenary Year

(Above) The trailer caravan — a house on wheels facilitating yet a further incursion of the countryside by the middle classes.

Then, quite suddenly, with the return to power of the Conservative Stanley Baldwin, the political tone of the magazine changed. Cast by *Country Life* as the "great healer", he was seen to personify a national rejection of the "foolishness of experiment". The editorials form a steady stream on the need for harmony between employer and employed and for "a truce to class warfare". "All the finer things in our civilisation", which were at stake during the General Strike of 1926, were rescued by Baldwin. These had been troubled years which witnessed a massive slump, huge unemployment and Britain's withdrawal from the Gold Standard. But even though recovery was evident from 1935 onwards, the signals were already in place that another war was on its way.

The unstable political atmosphere of the inter-war years explains the magazine's relentless emphasis on both urban and rural working class housing projects. Housing was seen as the key to averting working class discontent. The war had barely been over a month when the magazine declared that bad housing led to Bolshevism and to "social upheaval". Two themes then begin to unfold: how to modernise old cottages and how to build small new houses using new materials like concrete and with steel-

(Opposite) Car-ownership became common throughout the middle classes in the 1920s.

THE COTTAGE

HOUSING FOR COUNTRY PEOPLE CONTINUED TO BE A PREOCCUPATION THROUGH THE INTER-WAR YEARS. THE MAGAZINE ARGUED FOR A TRADITIONAL COTTAGE. THESE EXAMPLES IN DORSET WERE OF CONCRETE WITH A PLASTER RENDERING.

framed windows which were not only cheap, but which met with the magazine's aesthetic approval. None of these problems were easy to solve, for the war had left a "legacy of high costs, labour troubles, and a great shortage of certain materials … we want hundreds of thousands of houses, we want them quickly, and we want them at the lowest possible cost".

A steady flow of articles on houses built of concrete, weather-boarding and *pisé de terre* followed. In the end, *Country Life* opted, without any visible enthusiam, for concrete. "A flat-roof colony of cottages is in itself a queer thing when set down in the English countryside", wrote R. Randal Philips about examples seen at Silver End in Braintree, Essex, "and the first experimental pair make me feel uneasy that there is a deficiency somewhere." Colourwash and gardens, he believed, might enhance them: "they are honest and sound, and, I am told, very comfortable to live in. Yet, withal, they do not please the eye." And that was it. They are now regarded as the *incunabula* of the modern movement.

This attitude continued throughout the inter-war years. In London, where there was a need for some 30,000 houses: "we find delightful estates, well-planned". Christopher Hussey lauded Lutyens' vast blocks of working class flats between Vincent Square and Horseferry Road in 1930: "the most comfortable, sensible, light-flooded, and essentially modern block of buildings to found in England — or in Europe either, for that matter". By 1934, it was recorded that between 1918 and 1930, 178,000 people had been rehoused but that 1,240,000 were still waiting. No praise was too high for the priority given by national government to its relentless campaign to remove what were seen as the breeding grounds of social revolution. These pages illustrating lower class housing sit incongruously in the context of features about ancient manor houses and the wilder excesses of Art Deco. Viewed together, they provide idiosyncratic evidence of a will to accommodate the new order of things by the old established classes.

The revolution in government thinking, which succeeded in averting violent social reaction, is also vividly traced by the arrival of the estate column in 1918. For the next ten years, it provides a most compulsive read. It opened with the final flurry of land sales made up of the outlying parts of estates such as those run by the Westminsters at Eaton or the Thorndon estate of Lord Petre. These land sales were often made directly to tenants, as with Lord Aberdeen's Haddo estate. In January 1928, the column reviewed the previous decade and concluded that in 1919 "the sale of land peaked but from then on it fell off".

Increased production needed to be maintained to ensure good wages for the farmworker, a good income for the farmer, an excellent turnover for traders as well as an abundant food supply for the consumer. These wartime rates of production could only be maintained by the state's support of research, education, transport and housing together with other rural amenities. Agriculture needed to be mechanised in order to reduce manpower costs and bring prices down to meet outside competition. The optimism of *Country Life* in its editorials was to prove short-lived, for the confrontation of labour and capital interests grew. 1919 was a year of widespread agricultural unrest, with farmworkers demanding high wages and a five and a half day week. A year later, their demands rose to a £3 per week wage plus allowances, and a working day which ended at 5pm. *Country Life* was unsympathetic.

These years of conflict were tipped in favour of urban interests with Lloyd George's repeal of the Corn Production Acts in 1921 which wiped out any protection that the farmer might have against the flood of cheap foreign food imports and the erosion of guaranteed adequate wages for farmworkers. "It should be remembered", an editorial warned, "that, were the Act simply repealed, agriculture will swing back again into its old state of neglect", which is precisely what happened. The price of wheat halved between 1920 and 1921, and farmers began to go bankrupt on a massive scale as a slump set in which was to last almost until the outbreak of war in 1939. All the same, *Country Life*'s sympathies certainly did not lie with the farmworker, whose wages plummeted. Its view was essentially that of the urban middle classes, who were all too aware of the importance of placating the urban proletariat with better housing and cheaper food. By the autumn of 1923, farmers were "reduced to desperation", and 1925 and 1926 were to prove even more disastrous. Again, between 1928 and 1931, the average price of all farm products fell by a third. By then, *Country Life* was pressing for some kind of protectionism, and the government's option in 1930 for the Imperial Preference in favour of Empire imports signalled its acceptance. A whole series of marketing boards for milk, pigs, bacon, potatoes and hops was established. Nonetheless, in February 1937, the government was fiercely attacked for the terrible state of agriculture. "What would happen if war came?" people asked, and it was the realisation of the likely answer which was to accelerate a volte-face in attitudes.

For landowners who had seen their social and political power eroded, an economic squeeze followed. Income from land collapsed: although landowners had been able to raise rents after 1918, with the repeal of the Corn Production Acts in 1921, these fell by as much as 50%. By 1930, land was only worth what it had cost in 1850. The ratchet of taxation was turned even harder. Between 1919 and 1930, death duties rose to 40%: four years later, they reached 50%. In April 1925, *Country Life* spelt out the landowners' situation:

DRAWINGS OF COTTAGES

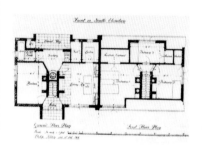

ONE OF A SERIES OF DRAWINGS MADE IN 1919 DEMONSTRATING HOW A COTTAGE COULD BE EXACTLY THE SAME ON THE INSIDE BUT HOW ITS EXTERIOR COULD BE ADAPTED TO FIT IN WITH THE EXISTING LOCAL VERNACULAR ARCHITECTURE.

(Above) Kitchens only began to appear after 1918, as the upper classes lost their servants. Saving labour became a constant theme.

He [the landowner] is usually the moral and responsible head of his own little community, the pioneer of new or improved methods of farming, the provider of better cottages and conditions, the improver of livestock, and frequently the breeder of bloodstock … Besides the management of his estate, the landowner is expected to act in various capacities in the county … In addition, he frequently maintains an historic house, the upkeep of which alone is a heavy burden …

The estate column provides dramatic evidence of the consequences of these momentous changes: the roll call of great houses to let is in itself a revelation. It opened in April 1919 with Levens Hall. Two years later, the following were available: Ragley Hall, Leeds Castle, Corsham Court, Knole, Mottisfont, Rousham, Blickling, Combe Abbey and Naworth Castle. Lord Spencer closed Althorpe owing to the "exorbitant cost of living, including onerous taxation". In 1922, the Duke of Northumberland closed Alnwick Castle. "I am, like so many other people," he said, "obliged to take measures of retrenchment owing to the excessively heavy burden of taxation." Letting was only a reprieve from facing up to the cruel realities of the new age. Many could not afford even that luxury, and sold up entirely.

In 1920, Trerice, Denham Place, Caversham Park, Godmersham Park, Quenby, Witley Court and five Welsh castles were all on the market. Thomas Hope's Deepdene became a hotel. Stowe was stripped. In 1923, Mereworth, Albury Park, Claremont, Swakeleys, Brocket Hall and West Wycombe Park followed suit. Brocket Hall was withdrawn after only one bid of £44,000.

At the same time, the sale of the contents of country houses began to escalate. Whole rooms were gutted as these sales included not only moveables such as pictures, furniture and tapestries, but their fittings as well. The three hundred lots in the Costessy Hall sale in 1920 included the oak-panelled chapel, its altar and pews. The dissolution of a centuries-old way of life is recorded before the reader's very eyes.

Even though these events appeared issue after issue, they were set side by side with the sunlit perspective of pages illustrating an endless stream of country houses which offered no hint of the crisis within, even though the pictures on closer inspection reveal the telling physical state of some of these buildings.

Despite this, the magazine's prosperity continued because it cleverly appealed to a readership which not only included the landowning classes, but also those from the aspiring middle classes for whom there was never a shortage of country houses of manageable size.

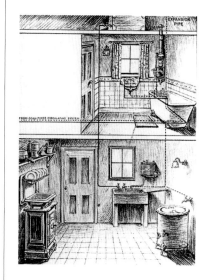

SINK BOILER

BY 1919, HOT-WATER COULD
BE SUPPLIED BY GAS.

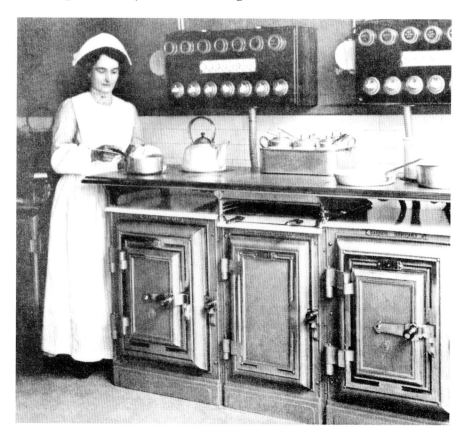

(Left) Cooking by electricity and gas replaced the old coal-fired ranges. Here a cook tends an early electric range in 1920.

Design for Living

The first indication in *Country Life* that there was no return to the traditional arrangement of country house living came in June 1920 in an article entitled, 'Modernizing Old Country Houses'. Looking back to the years before 1914, it reads:

> These were large, fat days of abundant cheap labour — times which now have definitely come to an end. The present owners are now faced with the business of taking in hand these wonderful, picturesque, rambling old houses and seeing how they can eliminate the unnecessary labour involved in running them while still preserving their beauty and essential English character.

The anonymous author goes on to discuss seven different means of achieving this, ranging from simplifying and altering room functions and eliminating passages to introducing modern light and central heating.

Five years later, the old stalwart Avray Tipping, demonstrating that he was able to move with the times, wrote on 'How to Live in the Great House — Old Houses and Labour Saving'. The article had been triggered by a visit to Woodhall, Hertfordshire, and he outlined how he would rearrange the rooms of the house to make it work with far fewer staff. This involved abandoning the basement and moving the kitchen onto the ground floor next to the dining room; shutting off the large formal reception rooms in order to retreat to a suite of smaller, more easily-heated rooms on one side of the house. Henceforth servants, even if they could be afforded, had to be courted since they would not put up with the traditional accommodation in the attic or basement. In 1922, R. Randal Philips discussed how to remodel town houses to operate with fewer servants, pointing out that in "providing suitable quarters we think of lifts and up-to-date equipment, well lit workaday rooms, adequate arrangements for heating and hot water supply …"

An unending series of articles on bathrooms, kitchens, central heating and other gadgetry filled the pages of the magazine's supplements. The display rooms of the new Electricity Board at the suitably-named Touchbutton House in Oxford Street became a Mecca and the awe-inspiring possibilities of this modern energy source were eulogised in an article entitled 'The Magic of Electricity' where "Many buttons make light work". The United States was heralded as the precursor of the new, servantless age: "this new condition of affairs has demanded that the house throughout and its working portion especially, shall be planned and equipped to enable the daily tasks to be carried out with the least possible amount of labour". By 1922, Professor C. H. Reilly was counselling those buying a country house to

(Opposite) Herbert Farjeon's bitter satirical poem on the destruction of historic London is framed within a collage of demolished buildings, among them the great town houses of the aristocracy.

PULLING DOWN LONDON
A TRACT FOR THE TIMES

OH, a fisherman's life is a life that's gay
　　As he sails on the open sea,
And a vagabond's life on the great highway
　　Is a life that is fine and free,
The steeplejack and the blacksmith black
　　Rejoice in their employment,
But a job I've got that tops the lot
　　For open-air enjoyment,
　　　　　As here
　　　　　I stand
　　　　My pick-axe in my hand,
　　　　　'Neath God's
　　　　　Blue sky
　　　I make the plaster fly—

Pulling down London, smashing up the town,
　　That is the life for me,
A-breaking up of beauty and a-knocking of
　　　　it down,
　　Under the sky so free,
　　　So whack that roof and bang those walls,
　　　　And scatter the old brickbats,
　　　And down with the Adelphi, and the
　　　　Temple and St. Paul's,
　　　And up with the service flats,
　　　　　By Gee,
　　　Yes, up with the service flats.
Sir Christopher Wren was all right then,
　　But he ain't no great shakes now,
So drill that drill, my lads, until
　　You can't see the dust for row.
Oh, the face of the world is changing fast,
But only fossils want things to last,
So shiver the foundations and blast the past,
　　　　Pulling down London Town.

If aeroplanes with bombs on high
　　Destroyed what I destroy,
Oh, wouldn't there be a great outcry,
　　You bet there would, my boy.
　　If what them Adam Brothers built
　　　Was bashed by the foe's barrage,
　　Oh, wouldn't we shout about the guilt
　　　Of doing it free of charge,
　　　　By Gee,
　　　Foreign labour free of charge !
But who will grouse if Pembroke House
　　Is bust by an Englishman,
Or shake his fist if I assist,
　　At the death of the best Queen Anne.
There's not much money in the past that's gone,
But there's oodles in a bran-new Odeon,
So civilisation marches on,
　　　Pulling down London town!
　　　　　　　HERBERT FARJEON.

Verses reproduced by permission from "Nine Sharp" at the Little Theatre

THE LADIES' HEY-DAY

FEMALE FASHION WAS A FEATURE OF COUNTRY LIFE FROM ITS EARLIEST DAYS, AS HERE WITH ASCOT LADIES' DAY.

(Opposite) Between the two world wars, Country Life *embraced modernism, here represented by the entrance hall to Claridge's Hotel with its superb Marion Dorn carpet.*

make generous provision for any staff: a maid should now have her own sitting room. As a consequence, country houses shrank in size, and in London the exit from the town house to the mews house and flat began, at a time when the lack of servants was the principal agent of change in interior decoration. In 1926, in 'A Plea for the Modern Spirit in Decoration in England', a condemnation of the work of Philip Webb, William Morris and their followers led to the statement that "the principal influence [on interior style] is probably lack of service. A house decorated in the modern spirit minimises labour." The reader was exhorted to throw out all mouldings and cornices and to thin out the furniture and knick-knacks in favour of "rest and space" and so save on cleaning. Six years earlier, J. E. Cloag had urged everyone to sweep out anything which smacked of the Victorian era. By 1923, this exhortation had become evangelical in its fervour:

> Let the surface of the paint be seen. Hang a few pictures and select them. They will look the better for the amount of light you will gain. Light lends brightness to the room after all, and we do not want a reversion to the Victorian age of ugly violently patterned papers and heavy curtains full of dirt and dust.
> Get rid of the heaviness and let in the light.

Such exhortations to toss out the old and embrace the new were ambiguous in a magazine which relied on salerooms and antique dealers for advertising revenue. Nonetheless, all through the 1920s, there runs a paradoxically bitter condemnation of the worship of the old, the cult of antiques and the continuing demand for reproduction period furniture. By 1929, Christopher Hussey was so entranced by all things new that he could write about the town house built by the architect Paul Paget stating that it fulfilled Le Corbusier's brief of being a machine for living in from which all period atmosphere and decoration had been eliminated: "The criterion of everything is not 'does it look nice?' but 'is it efficient? is it comfortable?'"

While Hussey and his colleagues relentlessly reported all things new, the space allotted to the traditional steadily multiplied, perhaps in response to the passing of the age of the great landowners when the contents of their country houses came onto the market. In 1921, *Country Life* started covering auction houses for the first time. The number of 'Pages for the Connoisseur' began to expand as a whole team of writers on antiques covered every conceivable aspect of the decorative arts: ceramics, silver, furniture, metalwork, textiles and glass. There is no doubt that the break-up of the country house collections stimulated interest and serious research in these areas by writers such as Percy Macquoid, Ralph Edwards, W. G. Thomson, Margaret Jourdain and William King. Antiques and collectables were now to be displayed in new ways: cabinets of porcelain were lit by elec-

(Right) Under Hussey, Country Life, *staged the Exhibition of Industrial Design in the Home in 1933. This room setting was by Sir Ambrose Heal.*

tricity, and tapestries were cut up to make cushions. Trend-setters like the Sitwells or Cecil Beaton ransacked junk shops for fragments of the past and deployed an arresting decor which tended to be ignored by the magazine. The financial uncertainties of the period also fuelled public interest in antiques: in 1931, the first editorial advocating investment in them appeared. A year later, in April, followed the words: "From well chosen works of art a man is assured an income." In January 1933, the buoyancy of the art market is commented upon: works of art "represent a form of investment that is comparable to the highest class of trustee security". Significantly, it was precisely at this period that the annual Grosvenor House Antiques Fair began.

The need to modernise contemporary domestic living arrangements, however, pre-occupied other writers in the magazine. Already in November 1923, an editorial chastised those who only looked back as opposed to those who reached to the future: "we have … to formulate anew the principles that unchangingly govern satisfying design …" But it was not to be until the early 1930s that the appalling quality of British design in the face of competition from Sweden, France and Germany became glaringly obvious. In March 1931, the level of design in manufactured products at the British Industries Fair was declared to be humiliating, and the need for a revolution in training along the lines of the German Werkbund, a co-operative of designers and craftsmen dedicated to producing the best in the way of every day artifacts, proclaimed. We needed, it was stated, a British equivalent of the Bauhaus, and state intervention to bolster the faltering economy and promote good taste.

These foreign design exhibitions left a great imprint on the younger generation. The idea of holding such an exhibition to display British modern design went back to 1923, when Chermayeff and Etchells, Le Corbusier's translator, tried, but failed, to establish one in the aftermath of *Country Life*'s sponsorship of the first Architecture Club exhibition. The idea was not to be resurrected until after the 1930 Stockholm Exhibition of Modern Industrial and Decorative Art and a Swedish Industrial Arts and Crafts exhibition at Dorland Hall in Regent Street the following year. Christopher Hussey had visited Germany in 1930 and 1931, and revived the notion that the magazine should sponsor such an exhibition. His powers of persuasion over the conservative Edward Hudson must have been considerable.

Hussey was the exhibition's chairman, with Frank Pick his deputy, and the young up-and-coming architect, Oliver Hill, also deeply involved. In general, the arts and crafts were to be excluded and the emphasis, reflecting the new democratic age, was to be on mass-manufactured items for the

(Below) Another room setting, this time by Hussey's friend, Oliver Hill, in the Exhibition of Industrial Design in the Home, 1933.

THE MODERN
EXAMPLE

AMYAS CONNELL'S RADICALLY
MODERN DESIGNS FOR
HIGH AND OVER, AMERSHAM,
BUCKINGHAMSHIRE.

home: furniture, pottery, glass, textiles, metalwork and graphics. The problem, it was recognised, was that whereas in Europe the main impact of William Morris and the Arts and Crafts Movement had been to lead to a design renaissance in manufacture, in Britain it had gone in the opposite direction. Here it had fuelled a sterile anti-industrial aesthetic locked into a worship of natural materials and the hand-made.

The Exhibition of British Industrial Design in the Home opened in June 1933, at the same time that the World Economic Conference was being held in London. Simultaneously, a consortium of avant-garde designers was launched under the name Unit One, with an aim to remedy "the lack of structural purpose" in English art. The magazine piled praise on the "splendour and beauty of Industrial Art", pinpointing a bungalow by Chermayeff and a "minimum flat" by Wells Coates at the design show. For the first time, manufacturers had agreed to be subject to selection and, as a consequence, "at last", wrote Arthur Oswald, "a common style is beginning to emerge". Following this, the government set up a council which included industrialists, designers, distributors and civil servants, with Frank Pick as chairman. In 1935, it was announced that there would be another exhibition, not at Dorland Hall, but at a far grander venue, the Royal Academy.

This exhibition of contemporary British art and industry, done in association with the Royal Society of Arts, was unfortunately relabelled "Art in Industry" when it eventually opened in 1935. Hussey, by then disenchanted with modernism, viewed the event as a disaster, and was deeply critical of its worship of what he regarded as false functionalism. He was to be equally critical of Oliver Hill's British Pavilion for the Paris Bicentennial Exhibition of 1937, and the close interest between *Country Life* and contemporary design ended in 1938 when it sponsored an exhibition on British country life, full of conversation pieces and sporting pictures, to which the new Queen came.

John Cornforth, himself a distinguished architectural editor of *Country Life*, explained Christopher Hussey's flirtation with modernism in terms of his interest in architecture. The magazine's influence at the time, Cornforth pointed out, was not to be underestimated, for it was taken by all those people who had the means to build and thus the ability to generate design style.

But even so, when the flood of beautiful houses which came onto the market after 1918 were advertised in *Country Life*, they were held up as the quintessence of the English ideal. The magazine provided information as to how to modernize them and printed articles on the restoration of a whole series of historic houses including Allington Castle, Ditchley and Trent Park. So, from the outset, any encouragement of the new was outweighed by the massive coverage of the old and how to adapt it for modern living.

Such circumstances did not bode well for the future of English domestic architecture on the grand scale. The building trade was in a terrible state with materials and labour becoming hugely expensive. In the future, houses could be nothing other than small and those few which were new came in a range of styles from the Jacobethan to the Beaux-Arts' neo-classical. In March 1920, C. H. B. Quennell, in reviewing Lawrence Weaver's second series of 'Small Country Houses of Today', lamented that "there is a hankering after the picturesque, an Elizabethan sort of outlook which is a little out of place these days".

Finding inspiration in England's architectural heritage became a central feature of the magazine's editorial policy: in 1923, *Country Life* sponsored the first exhibition of the newly formed Architecture Club, and Hussey lauded the work of Detmar Blow, Goodhart Rendel, Guy Dawber, Philip Tilden and Edward Maufe. Later, he cited Lutyens' Ednaston Manor "as nearly perfect a modern country house of its size as can be found in England". He sensed the lack of architectural direction afflicting his readership, with a cry from the heart: "Men look around in despair and see first one and then another of their cherished beliefs broken up … In art especially nobody knows where they are." He recognised that simplicity must be the key in the new technological age, but "'Modern' is an atrocious word. It not only connotes a superiority over every other age, but it is untrue …" The contemporary movement in art, he concluded, was retrogressive. His uneasiness at the drift of things is reiterated in his review of the next year's exhibition: "Life may become so rational and organised that we all have to live in machines as perfectly disciplined and as communal as hospitals or ships … architecture is reduced to pure utility — everything practical, sanitary and moving with a click …" Le Corbusier was a "brilliant, but slightly unbalanced, French architect".

Hussey's rather surprising choice of the only truly modern building in the exhibition was a group of utilitarian silos on a farm in Devon, "to our mind, the finest piece of architecture in the Exhibition". But the ambiguity of the magazine's stance was always apparent. While the architectural profession condemned the spread of the picturesque in the form of suburban half-timbered Tudor residential building, the magazine was less sure. Instead, a new national style was called for "in order to be more sensible, cheaper and healthier. But not in order to be modernist." The magazine's shift against modernism became stronger in 1931, in Hussey's account of High and Over in Amersham, Buckinghamshire, built by Amyas Connell. The client, Bernard Ashmole, demanded sun, protection from the wind, views to the surrounding landscape and that the house should harmonise with its surroundings. The local authorities had reluctantly granted plan-

THE LATEST LUXURY

CHARTERS, SUNNINGDALE, SURREY:
A MODERN PALACE, REPLETE
WITH ITALIANATE COLONNADES
AND MARBLE BATHROOMS.

(Above) High Cross Hill, Dartington, Devon, one of the startlingly up-to-date houses covered by Country Life *before Christopher Hussey's disenchantment with the modern movement.*

(Right) Interior of a flat in Gloucester Lodge, Regent's Park, London, designed by Robert Lutyens. A striking example of the integration of a new interior within the framework of an older building.

ning for this most uncompromising of modern houses, eulogized by Hussey as "a brilliant synthesis of contemporary thought with contemporary materials … in its clean lines and white walls there is nothing to conflict with the wide downland landscape in which it stands", a view which he later contradicted: "houses of this type can never fit into the English landscape in the same way as buildings constructed of local materials and in traditional styles".

It is difficult to believe Hussey's shift in attitude to modernism was not coloured by the traditionalist values of the class to which he belonged and it should be remembered that Hussey was writing from the stance of being a garden historian, and was the author of *The Picturesque*, published in 1927. His accounts of modernist houses are increasingly pessimistic.

In 1933, High Cross Hill at Dartington in Devon left him profoundly concerned:

> Habit, sentiment, associations, all bind us to a preference for the traditional type of home … These associations are not lightly to be dismissed, for, mixed up with a lot of sentiment that can safely be jettisoned, they comprise our heritage of humanist civilisation.

By 1934, the modernist "invasion" from the continent (now all too visible in the form of ever-increasing numbers of exiles from the Nazi regime) was evident in communal, rather than domestic, architecture, such as hospitals, schools, bridges and garages.

If modern architecture is to acquire a style worthy to be placed

(Above) Mulberry House, Westminster, London, built by Darcy Braddell with murals by Glyn Philpot. One of the stunning contemporary interior schemes publicised by Country Life.

in the succession of the great historic styles, the fundamental qualities of rhythym, proportion and harmony and those delicate nuances and refinements which attend them will have first to be reinstated.

In January 1938, Hussey returned with one final scourging attack:

> ... to the low-brow, the antagonistic, or even the commonplace lover of English scenery who feels vaguely that architecture has something to do with the soil and history, this affair of clicking wheels, diagrammatic silhouettes, and abstract shapes can scarcely fail to be puzzzling, if not repellent ...

The setting of the building was deemed to be the last consideration of the modernist architect: "It is essentially an urban industrial style, well adapted for towns with no particular character, but looking foreign to country landscape." Nonetheless, it was inevitable that modernism would triumph and be made manifest as the architecture of the Welfare State took hold.

Preserving Arcadia

The consequences of the social revolution in the years after 1918 were visibly evident in the physical appearance of the countryside. Concern for the latter had led to the creation of a series of societies whose purpose was to preserve open spaces, wildlife and antiquities: the Society for the Protection of Ancient Buildings (1877), The Society for the Protection of Birds (1889), the National Trust (1895) and others. These concerns were reflected in new laws such as the first Ancient Monuments Act of 1882 and the creation of the Royal Commission on Historic Monuments in 1908 which set for its concerns a terminal date of 1700, which was extended in 1921 to 1714 and in 1951 to 1850. The care and preservation of the countryside was one aspect which went back to *Country Life*'s earliest days. Bernard Darwin wrote that "there has always been a natural sympathy between *Country Life* and the National Trust" and that was to be enduring. The magazine had run a series of appeals to save land adjacent to the Trust's own acreage on Box Hill starting before 1914, and then in 1926 and 1935, which were ultimately successful.

The issue of preserving the countryside brought town dwellers, who saw it as an amenity reachable by new forms of transport and increased personal prosperity, into conflict with the preservationist lobby which united a wide social spectrum combining Fabian intellectuals, who saw the land as belonging to the people, and aristocrats, who wished things to stay as they had been in the past. Both sides tapped the pervasive cult of the rural idyll in a drive to halt the urban sprawl, and to create green belts and establish the National Parks. The farmer, later to be cast as the villain of the piece, was, during this period, seen as the heroic conserver of both social life and the vanishing beauties of the countryside.

By the middle of the 1920s, the pressures exerted on the countryside for land for housing and industry, symbolised by the incursion of vast electricity pylons within the landscape and the swallowing of acre after acre by the explosive growth of the suburbs, made it clear that some new form of organisation was called for to stem the erosion of the landscape. It was obvious that the National Trust was never going to be the militant protest movement of the kind that was desperately needed. *Country Life* instead took up the challenge: concern for the spoliation of the landscape first appeared in January 1920 in face of the threat to introduce dams and deep water courses all over Dartmoor by the promoters of the Hydro-Electrical Bill, a threat which was thwarted. In December 1925, the magazine supported the practice of zoning, that is, agreeing to allocate the land for either building or preservation, but these matters were as nothing compared to the

(Opposite) The saloon in Devonshire House, London, one of William Kent's masterpieces. The house never reopened after its closure during the war and was demolished in 1925 to be replaced by a block of flats.

(Right) Lutyens' neo-Georgian Ednaston
Manor, Derbyshire, was hailed by Hussey as
the perfect country house.

running battle to preserve the South Downs which began in the following year and which was to run on through the 1930s.

> Whoever has seen the debauch of cheap and vulgar exploitation on the most magnificent stretch of Downs between Brighton and Newhaven knows how England's green and pleasant land is being devastated. The motor bicycle and the small motor car have made possible the variegated paper bungalow in places fifty miles from town. Indeed, no corner of England is really safe.

Ribbon development had also arrived. In February 1926, the theme of the spoilation of rural England occurred again: "It is today ten chances to one that we alight upon a tin or asbestos bungalow or a choice assortment of hideous advertisement boards." Such sights, it added, were rare before 1914. "Now the case is entirely different. Kent and Essex are destroyed and Sussex is threatened."

These blasts formed a prelude to the establishment of the Council for the Protection of Rural England under the aegis of Patrick Abercrombie, Professor of Civic Design at Liverpool University, and the architect Guy Dawber. The Council became a reality in December 1926, but during the months leading to its launch, its firmest ally was *Country Life*. In July, it sounded the death knell of the village shop: "Our villages have been invaded by the great multiple shops from the cities, controlled and managed by 'foreigners' ..." In August, it wrote of the need for the Council for "preserving village scenery at the same time that the houses are brought up to modern requirements". The Council's role was to co-ordinate and inspire regional planning and at its launch, *Country Life* spelt out the urgent need for the

> ... education of the public in what, for want of a better term,
> we must call the art of landscape design, and better use of
> existing, and creation of new, powers of control ... *Country
> Life* has always stood for the use of the country in work and
> leisure, and we maintain that the preservation of its beauty is
> compatible with economic development.

Much editorial coverage was given to the Council's earliest activities: at a conference at Reading on the subject of zoning in the Thames Valley, a passionate address by Guy Dawber concerned the wanton destruction of "the beauty and solemnity that our ancestors and Nature unassisted have given to our country ..." The main road to Salisbury beyond Middle Wallop, he lamented, is now "spattered with untidy shacks, garages and what are presumably chicken farms". The Town Planning Act of 1925, he concluded, had been a failure.

Stonehenge also came under threat with the proposed construction of an aerodrome, a garage and a café. The magazine launched an appeal on behalf of the National Trust. It was successful. Then, in June 1929, came the threat of electric pylons crossing the South Downs which became a reality following the Electric Board's argument that it was too expensive to bury them. A

(Left) Lutyens' additions to Penheale Manor House, Cornwall, epitomise the resilience of traditional architectural conventions throughout the 1920s and 1930s.

RIBBON DEVELOPMENT

SUBURBIA EXTENDED ITS TENDRILS
ACROSS THE LANDSCAPE IN 1935.
THE SERVICE ROADS LEADING OFF
THE GREAT WEST ROAD PROVIDED
THE FRAMEWORK FOR THE NEW
HOUSING ESTATES TO BE BUILT.

plea followed that they should not be allowed to cross the Lake District. In October, there was a note of urgency concerning the need to educate townfolk about: "the intrusion of ugliness, crudity where all was mellow, vulgarity where reigned simplicity, and ruthless utilitarianism where, if things had a purpose, they served it in a traditional manner." Then, in January 1930, an editorial led with a heading which used an expression which was to become all too familiar: 'The National Heritage'. The editorial was about Ramsay MacDonald's commission to examine the creation of National Parks, something which *Country Life* welcomed as long it did not mean that any of the land not included was to be abandoned to urbanisation. But National Parks were not established until after 1945.

The need for planning was paramount. Regional planning was "the modern name for … landscape gardening" and the newly created local authorities were cast as heirs to the aristocratic tradition. In May 1935, in the Silver Jubilee issue, there was a retrospective review of the state of the countryside now marred by "harsh new buildings, crude lines and noise". In a massive series the next year, there was a continuing tirade against a "spoliation" which had spawned "a huge suburbia" and "a new kind of abomination of desolation" with the conclusion that some new kind of National Planning Commission was called for to remedy the ineffectiveness of existing legislation and the founding of a central control structure within which the Society for the Protection of Ancient Buildings, the National Trust, the Ministry of Works and the various provisions of the Town and Country Planning Act could all play their roles.

Even though *Country Life* played an honourable part in these pioneering campaigns, it cannot be denied that the victories of the preservation movement were few and far between. The Labour government's attempt to control development in the countryside was thwarted by the Lords after the 1931 election, the same event which saw the sidelining of the proposal to create National Parks. The 1935 Ribbon Development Act, which forbade the building of houses less than two hundred feet from a main road was a moderate victory in the context of the increasing urban sprawl which seemed an inevitable consequence of social democracy.

Preservation did not only concern the landscape but also buildings, both large and small. The drive to demolish slum accommodation resulted in the massive loss of early English domestic architecture from medieval, Tudor and early Stuart periods. Under the Housing Act of 1919, it was local medical officers who had the power to condemn a building as being unfit for human habitation, and, through that decision, precipitate its demolition. Although local rural authorities had powers to save old cottages in villages and recondition them (as was fervently advocated by *Country Life*), they rarely invoked them. In February 1927, Stanley Baldwin, true to his belief in the rural dream, spoke to the Royal Society of Arts of the necessity to preserve old cottages, and provoked the magazine to write:

> From its earliest days *Country Life* has pleaded the cause of preservation [this was not quite true], and it is pleading still ... Its advocacy has been enlisted alike for churches and bridges, for town houses and country seats. But often and again it has insisted on the beauty and value of the English village and hamlet ... [but the fact that] the evil spirit still lives and flourishes is only too evident to those who move along country roads and see the planless dotting of inadequate and vulgar bungalows and cottages that hideously spot the pleasant vales and hills of England.

Two months later there was a return to the subject with a *de haut en bas* rebuke for where "stock patterns are used, such as imitation timbered gables, that appeal to the rising lower classes". Land for such development was indeed cheap in the 1920s and 1930s due to the agricultural slump, and in face of the demand for small houses by the hugely-expanding middle classes, whole areas were swamped forever in the Home Counties, the South coast, the coasts of Devon and Cornwall and parts of the Midlands. In July 1925, *Country Life* again thundered:

> ... all over the country thousands of bungalows and cheap houses are springing up — badly built, badly designed, devastating the landscape ... The result is a menace to the countryside, a menace to the cause of decent architecture, and a menace to the householders themselves ...

But there was little that could be done, even after the Ribbon Development Act.

Country Life also fought the preservation battle in the city. Most of it concerned London. This started in 1920 with the proposal to demolish nineteen Wren churches in the City: "they are unique; they are precious heritages from the past which this generation cannot barter away without incurring the condemnation of present and future generations", the magazine stated. These years witnessed the wreck of Regent Street at the hands of the Crown Commissioners, the demolition of Soane's Bank of England ("deplorable, almost heart-rending", Avray Tipping wrote) and the loss of London squares to commercial development. One by one, these squares ceased to be residential and became offices. In some cases, the depradation was even more serious as in the case in Bloomsbury, where the open spaces in the middle of squares and crescents were actually built over. The demolition of the Foundling Hospital was also a major cause for deep regret: "It is

THE ROADSIDE BUNGALOW

RIBBON-DEVELOPMENT HOUSING SPRANG UP ALL OVER BRITAIN DURING THE 1940S AND 1950S. IT WAS THE GOVERNMENT'S ATTEMPT TO CONTROL THE INCREASING URBAN SPRAWL.

preservation still remained a minority issue. It was during these years that *Country Life* established a role that it still occupies today as the unofficial mouthpiece of the preservation movement. Its greatest energies were, however, to be reserved for what was the mainstay of every issue — the country house. The story of their preservation began when, on 7th June 1919, only a year after the war ended, there appeared the following major editorial:

> A survey creates an impression of a general exodus from the stately homes of England. Peer and squire, knight and lady, are forsaking the halls, gardens and grounds which, in many cases, were built or laid out centuries ago ... We are not so advanced, or Bolshevik, if you will, as to feel no regret that these ancient insitutions should be shattered ... People anticipate that as the Labour Party becomes stronger, its attacks on land will increase in violence, and consequently possession of land will be odious. Prudence steps in, too, and shows that the present is an excellent time at which to get rid of property ... as the ... expense of merely owning an estate grows annually. It is a concrete object of wealth, and therefore subject to all the tributes in the shape of rates, taxes, income tax and tithe which can be heaped on it, and this to say nothing of the final act of spoliation, the costly Death Duties. Further, the cost of repairs and mortgage interest have increased and are increasing to such an alarming extent that he may not in all instances have the wealth to keep the place going.

(Right) London's Georgian and Regency squares came under increasing pressure for redevelopment as commercial premises.

THE ENGLISH ARCADIA

(Above) The saloon of Norfolk House, London, a rococo masterpiece, demolished in 1937.

But there was no special pleading for government action on preservation, and the loss of country houses through the 1920s was accepted. Most of the houses found buyers, demolitions were rare and alternate use was common. In 1922, for example, Brancepath Castle was offered by Lord Boyne as a branch hospital, Rendlesham Hall became another and Canford Hall took on a new lease of life as a girls school. Those near London or along the South coast were acquired by developers, the house sold off and the land built over. In the same year, the new owner of Rushbrooke Hall threatened to demolish it and on 21st October, the magazine stated in its 'A Sign of the Times':

> Obedient to the pressure of heavy taxation our bigger country houses are regretfully being evacuated one by one, and being transformed ... from houses, in every real old-fashioned sense of the word, to far-fetched and alien purposes.

In 1927, the new owner of Swakeleys approached the National Trust and the Society for the Protection of Ancient Buildings, who came up with a

(Above) Philip Tilden's dramatic terracing at Sir Philip Sassoon's house Port Lympne, Kent, would seem to owe more to Hollywood than Georgian England.

(Opposite) The Painted Room at Port Lympne by Rex Whistler. A tented room with an architectural capriccio typical of 1930s romanticism.

scheme for its survival, but nothing happened. The following year the fate of Knole provoked another major editorial on the subject. Contrasting the hard realities facing country house owners with the irony of having a Prime Minister, Baldwin, who promulgated a vision of the English rural idyll, the magazine commented: "It is exceedingly unjust and short-sighted that one who inherits such a place should pay Death Duties on a house and park which is regarded even by him as national property." Knole was a "great home maintained at private expense for public pride and enjoyment". But the only concession allowed them was the exclusion of scheduled heirlooms from probate. The magazine continued:

> Houses of the type mentioned above [of the ilk of Hardwick, Chatsworth and Burghley] are history still alive and present among us … they are everything that a museum, at great cost, subsequently tries, and fails completely, to re-create: a home in which the finest works of art and traditions of the past are still an integral part of life. Everything possible should be done to prevent, not to expedite, their sale and the dispersal of their contents. Their occupants should be recognised, as they recognise themselves, as trustees of national property and historic

A COUNTRYMAN AT HEART

monuments ... Such houses, their contents and parks, should be entirely relieved from Death Duties, local rates and taxes, and be recognised for what they are: priceless national possessions ...

After this resounding salvo, the subject went off the boil for some years, apart from an unusual piece in 1932 by Patrick Balfour, entitled 'How to save our Country Houses'. Way ahead of its time, its contents must have come as something of a shock to its conservative readers: "Our country house life, from a tourist point of view, is the biggest commercial asset we possess. Why, then, do we not commercialise it?" The response to that call was to come only after 1945, when the Duke of Bedford and the Marquess of Bath swung open their gates to the public.

The great turning point in the preservation debate was Lord Lothian's address to the National Trust in 1934, an event generously covered by the magazine in the issue of 28th July. The speech was an appeal to both the Trust and the government to co-operate in constructing a framework to preserve "a national possession that has now become unique in the world" as "the most characteristic contribution of this nation to civilised life". *Country Life*, one was informed, had compiled a list of some six to seven hundred of the most important country houses with a supplementary listing of the sixty greatest which should be preserved. It is interesting that this desire to preserve them extended beyond their physical fabric and environs to include "as far as might be, the kind of life they stand for".

Much debate ensued as to how this was to be achieved and what the owners should give as some form of quid pro quo, with the example of La Demeure Historique in France cited as a precedent. The Finance Bill of 1937, which exempted from death duty houses which were made over to the National Trust but which also preserved the right of tenancy by the family, was debated in detail within the columns of *Country Life*. The solution to the debate was anticipated by Sir Charles Trevelyan's bequest of Wallington to the Trust in 1936 on terms which included an endowment for its future maintenance. Although this act provided a model for the saving of country houses, there was no initial rush to emulate it by other such owners. Any hopes they might have had that the government would come through with some form of tax remission to relieve them vanished when the defence of the realm rose to the top of the agenda, thus ruling out any tax relief for the foreseeable future for those who clearly belonged to the privileged classes. And so, by the late 1930s, a sense of poignant loss and tragedy concerning the fate of the country house predominated the magazine.

The need to be sensitive about democratic feeling, was recognised by both government and magazine alike, especially as confrontation with

Germany seemed increasingly likely. Already in 1933, *Country Life* had registered its "revulsion" at the Hitler's coming to power, with his ideas and policies which "can only lead to war". Although a solitary aberration, the magazine ran an article on 'Hitler as a Countryman' in March 1936. A month later, his occupation of the Rhineland precipitated the comment that, should Britain fail to honour her obligations under the Treaty of Versailles of 1918, "we should be indelibly disgraced". By then, the Territorial Army had been revived and pointers were given as to "the vital part which must be played [by agriculture] in any future war …" The Defence Department began to take land over and the Air Raid Precaution Department was established. In March 1938, the term "The Home Front" made its appearance, and defeat was "certain without it". The Home Guard followed, and in October, a chaotic rehearsal of the evacuation of children. During 1939, air raid shelters were delivered and, early in September, war came at last. On 2nd September, the editorial 'The Faith for the Future' cast the impending struggle as one between the cult of state nationalism and liberty. The future, it was stated, could only lie in a "United Democratic States of Europe". Considering the magazine's insular outlook, its loyalty to Crown and Empire, both of whose virtues it regularly celebrated, this statement was a surprising anticipation of the European Union.

Baldwin's advocacy of the rural myth was, it turned out, a shrewd political gamble, for it united people during a period of profound social upheaval and offered all classes a common ground on which they could meet. The rural myth was also a convenient vehicle for the topical emphasis on Britishness and Englishness which was explored in great detail by various publications: in 1927, *The Countryman* was founded; in 1929 Longmans began its *English Heritage* series; in 1930 Batsford began two other series along the same lines, *English Life* and *British Heritage*; and H. V. Morton's *In Search of England*, published in 1927, went through sixteen editions. Arthur Bryant, in his *The English National Character* in 1934, wrote that despite the fact that most people were now town dwellers, they had been mainly countryfolk only three generations before: "our subconscious selves hark back to their instincts and ways of life", he added. Beyond the blot of the Industrial Revolution lay, he believed, "the sunlight of the green fields from which we came".

The realities of country life in 1939 were, of course, far removed from such poetic reveries: it remained hard, ridden with drought, poverty, appalling housing and depression. The squire and the larger of the far-mowners still dominated the rural population. But the vision Baldwin supported remained central to the nation's consciousness as it entered another devastating war.

THE EMERGENCY SHELTER

THIS HUT, ADVERTISED IN SEPTEMBER 1939, WAS TO PROTECT READERS FROM HITLER'S BOMBS.

Isolation

The magazine's reaction to the declaration of war in 1939 was exactly the opposite from what it had been under Hudson's auspices in 1914. The decision as to how it was to be treated (or rather not treated) must have been taken by Christopher Hussey at its outbreak. His editorial policy for what turned out to be the next five years was enuniciated in the 16th September issue:

> … it is our purpose to continue to produce a paper that shall reflect the spirit and the substance of the England that exists in moor and downland, in mansion and hamlet, in the ploughed field and the swift-running beck … It will reflect, but only as circumstances demand, the incursion of the atmosphere of war into the realm: it has, through half-a-century, made peculiarly its own, the realm which embraces the whole gamut of those things which are the substance of our culture and the background of what is best in English life. It will continue to illustrate and describe the homes, and the sports and pastimes of country-loving folk, the way of the bird in the air, the life of field and forest …

And thus it was to be. Inevitably, as wartime restrictions bit deeper, the issues shrank dramatically until the magazine was but a shadow of its peacetime form. In 1942, the number of copies which could be printed was limited and the paper shortage precipitated a change in design in which as much as possible was crammed on to each page. A huge range of subjects vanished, including motoring (a fruitless topic owing to petrol rationing), gardening (apart from the odd piece on vegetable growing), fashion and the theatre. What Hussey retained reflected what he viewed as representing "the spirit and the substance of England": old houses, photographed without any hint of the deprivations of war; nature; antiques; golf and agriculture. The latter figured in a substantial way, for if the war impinged at all, it was in the continuous and massive coverage of increased food production. Otherwise, as Bernard Darwin, the chronicler of the magazine's first fifty years, wrote, *Country Life* went through the war with almost only one or two photographs of bomb damage.

The magazine thus offered a war-weary public a conceptual retreat from the present reality of bombs falling, destroyed cities and battlefield reports. In 1941, when Mass Observation, the pioneer public-opinion organisation, asked people "What does Britain mean to you?", towns hardly appeared in any reply: people were fighting for an essentially rural vision of Britain. The staple visual diet of *Country Life*, with its rolling hills and village greens, timeless and indestructible, served propaganda purposes which favoured the

(Opposite) Lady Harris as Chief Commandant, Auxiliary Territorial Service — one of the few visual concessions Country Life *made to the Second World War.*

(Above) Images in the magazine such as this — the white cliffs of Dover — had a special poignance in time of war, and echoed the spirit of heroic defiance which was supported by the media in general.

existence of a mythical Britain. The crisis of 1940, far from shattering faith in the rural idyll, only reinforced it as the touchstone of national identity. Winston Churchill recognised the value of presenting the war as a struggle between Britain, a humane, old-fashioned rural culture, against Germany, a heartless industrial society run amok. The myth of an almost pastoral democracy, already used to such effect by Baldwin to paper over the cracks of social division, became even more dominant as the war threw people together, levelling the class system out even further. That myth maintained its spell: a widow writing to Christopher Hussey after her husband's death in North Africa recorded that "he said he found a copy of *Country Life* … and that it was so lovely to read what one what was fighting for".

On 24th August 1940, when the Battle of Britain was being waged, an issue was dedicated to the "core of the English spirit" highlighting in its pages "something of the face of the land that her sons and grandsons are now mustered to defend …" There was H. V. Morton on 'The New "Merry England"', gazing down from a church tower and meditating on the panorama of landscape and village. There was Christopher Hussey on 'The Englishman's Home' ("all tell of continuous liberty and love"), A. L. Rowse on 'The English Spirit' ("Happy contentment", "the secret compact … with nature", "pride, courage, tenacity") and G. C. Taylor celebrating the garden tradition of Robinson and Jekyll.

The practical effects of the war on the countryside were immediately apparent when it came to farming, for it turned overnight from being in a slump to playing a central role within the war effort. There was a huge drive to plough up all available land, modernising farming in the process, for it enforced mechanisation at last, an improvement which came in handy as not only had the farmworkers gone to the war but those who were left were attracted to the factories which offered far better wages. Until 1939, as agricultural labour was so cheap, there had been no incentive to mechanise, but in May 1942, the magazine noted that: "From agricultural anarchy we have passed, in two years, to the most drastic system of war-time control of farming that this country has ever known."

In response to the drift of farmworkers to the city, the government intervened by enforcing the direction of labour and by introducing subsidy, the latter thereby setting the pattern for what was to happen after 1945. *Country Life* surveyed the agricultural situation county by county and went on to print a series on what was happening on some of the great estates such as Badminton and Gorhambury. As early as January 1941, writers wondered what would happen after the war. The bitter betrayal of 1921, when the government reneged on the famers opening up the country to a flood of cheap imported food, was still vividly in people's minds, and they were wary of similar events: "A prosperous countryside is ... a political and social asset to a nation at all times ..." By 1942, the future of the countryside was seen to be one in which increased state control and subsidy were to be central.

The future changes which people anticipated removed any chance of the slowing down of the wider social revolution which had taken effect in the inter-war years. During the war, the ideological groundwork for what was to be the post-war Welfare State was laid, from the Beveridge Report to the Education Act. Christopher Hussey, on reviewing the Rebuilding of Britain exhibition at the National Gallery in February 1943, actually described it as the visual equivalent of the Beveridge Report, one which had accepted the notion of a social revolution. It was clearly not one to which he warmed. The photographs of the buildings which this new age was to bring were, he deemed, "dreary".

The same story can be told in the case of the magazine's coverage of the proposals for rebuilding London. In October 1940 came *Country Life*'s solitary illustrated spread of bombed London buildings and two months later, there followed a series on the "London that is to be", one which actually called for a radical post-war redistribution of its industry and population. A eulogy of Lutyens' vision of a new city with noble vistas to and from St Paul's was also made. Lutyens, "the greatest English architect of our time", however, died in 1944, the same year in which a very different exhibition was staged showing what actually was to happen to the bombed City. The vistas around the great cathedral were still just apparent in the new plans, and there was some control of the height of the buildings in proximity to it, but the proposals were pronounced as "unimaginatively competent" by the magazine.

Design was to evoke the same negative response. In October 1944, a new government body was set up "to further improvement in the design of everyday things". Good and innovative design was seen to be central to any post-war revival of British industry. In January 1945, the magazine welcomed the creation of the Council of Industrial Design, "the most constructive step yet taken in this country to raise standards of design in the produce of factory and mill". And yet, and here comes the revealing corollary, "the problem is, in a classless and part-educated society, where to find a substitute for the patron with the leisure to cultivate his and the public's taste".

There appeared a brave series on post-war country houses in 1941, with designs by a series of architects including the up-and-coming Frederick Gibberd. People would still, it opined, want to build them and there would continue to be service of sorts (one design included accommodation for a maid), but the general move was towards the use of multi-purpose living-

(Above) 'Little England' — here represented by the village of Kersey in Suffolk — became a central icon in the national consciousness and was celebrated by the magazine, where such images were common currency.

dining and kitchen-dining rooms. In July 1944, Christopher Hussey printed a conversation with Edwin Lutyens' architect son, Robert, on future country houses. It recognised that there would be no more ancestral houses: "owing to fluctuations of income between generations, and extensive recruitment to the possessing classes, on the one hand, and the gradual dispossession of the territorial families on the other". Nonetheless, Robert Lutyens could still envisage a house for a commuting businessman with eight to ten acres of land including two paddocks, a kitchen garden and a formal garden. Inside there would be day and night nurseries, one large living room, and an optional dining room, but he added that the kitchen was now the logical place in which to eat.

However, new country houses were to be the last thing needed in 1945. Instead, the urgency was for housing the returning servicemen and their families as well as the bombed-out civilian populace. In November 1943, it was reckoned that between four and five million new homes would be needed as soon as possible if "social tranquillity" was not to be jeopardized. In 1944, housing did indeed feature in the magazine as a major topic, with

(Below) Country houses were requisitioned for use by evacuees from the public schools. A state room at Blenheim Palace, Oxfordshire, has been transformed into a dormitory.

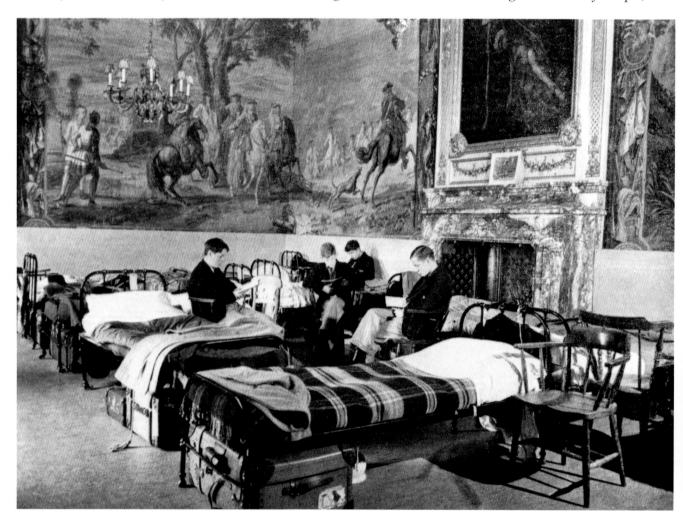

THE ENGLISH ARCADIA

(Left) 'Lady Carnarvon playing with Little People from the East End, at Highclere Castle.' A rare, if rather patronising, glimpse of refugee children.

the recognition that working-class housing now had to incorporate a far higher standard than ever before, and include modern plumbing and bathrooms. In October, there was a report on a series of specimen houses which had been built under the aegis of the Ministry of Works at Northolt. There was not much enthusiam for them due to their lack of variety, but the ones which caught the magazine's eye the most were those which were steel-framed and clad with concrete blocks. The magazine lamented that: "There will not be the time, labour, material or money ... to realise the more grandiose plans for the future ..."

The new era which beckoned brought with it at least one consolation: the cause of preservation could only take off, it was thought. The preservation of the countryside was seen as part of the "better Britain" post-war package and, in 1941, a Committee on Land Utilisation in Rural Areas was set up with Lord Justice Scott as its chairman. Its report endorsed the principles of the green belt, of containment, the creation of National Parks and nature reserves and subsidy for farming. Clough Williams-Ellis, writing in September 1941, viewed the era with greater optimism than the patrician Hussey, since he realised that the future of the countryside was to depend on the attitude of town dwellers whose education about the countryside was to be a priority:

> If history, and man-made beauty, manifested in noble architecture and fine craftsmanship is freely displayed and made familiar to an ever-widening audience, I believe that this wider

(Above) Child evacuees from Dr Barnardo's homes in the snow at Ripley Castle, Yorkshire, enjoying a country house sojourn.

public will come to consider these treasures as in some sort their own.

Williams-Ellis was almost anticipating the heritage culture which was to emerge in the 1970s.

The future of the infrastructure of the remaining aristocratic and gentry estates lay not only in the hands of the state but in those of the National Trust. In January 1945, G. M. Trevelyan celebrated that institution's half century, writing in *Country Life*: "we have a common cause, the rural and agricultural life and the natural and historic beauty of England". These were the years when the Trust's country house scheme began to work. Indeed, in a succession of articles, *Country Life* regarded the Trust as the only means whereby to ensure the survival of the great country houses into the new era (their use in wartime was only chronicled in a series on evacuated public schools), and the diaries of James Lees-Milne, the Trust's historic buildings secretary, were especially vivid in their picture of the decline into which these houses had fallen. All the same, novelists still cast the great country house as a place of reassuring security during the anguish of war. By the time Evelyn Waugh's *Brideshead Revisited* was published in 1945, such houses had caught the imagination of the educated classes, and made even the incoming Socialist government sympathetic to their plight.

In a series in 1945, entitled 'The Prospect before us', *Country Life* spelled out what the post-war age would bring. In the first of these articles, Christopher Hussey stated: "The English landscape is the greatest contribution to European art", the creation of landowners whose very existence guaranteed its survival. He lamented a vanished world and the fate which had overtaken the pictorial vision of the eighteenth century. That vision was "our greatest loss ... Yet it still persists among the more conservative elements of the nation ..."

These are the words of a man unhappy with the direction of his own age who believed that: "the devitalised countryside was economically dependant on the overgrown town, and would have been at the mercy of urban materialism but for the persistence, in the countryman, of an antiquated relic of the humanist past." He felt that:

> democracy has still to prove itself capable of the self-discipline and idealism required to undertake country planning and town building such as that found in the eighteenth century, with its firm grasp of humane values, discharged with such outstanding success ...

It was views such as these which firmly ensconced *Country Life* in the tranquil backwater it lounged in for the next two decades.

(Below) Binding by hand on a Lake District farm.

AUSTERITY

1945–1965

The Common Good

A New Iron Age

A Struggle to Survive

The Pastoral Preserve

The Common Good

On New Year's Day 1947, *Country Life* celebrated its golden jubilee with a dinner for four hundred guests at the Dorchester Hotel in London. The first of the three toasts was made by R. A. Butler and was to "The English Tradition". He began by saying that he read the magazine every Saturday evening, beginning with the advertisements. But then he struck a more serious note, praising the journal for enshrining within its covers ideals which crossed every social divide: "The very title of *Country Life* represented … the essence of our island tradition … a journal which portrayed country things and country ways and depicted beauty in the many forms in which it embellished and enriched English homes." Coming from a Conservative politician, it is hardly surprising to find him articulating the ideology put forward by Stanley Baldwin. The editorial which accompanied the jubilee issue also dwelt on what *Country Life* believed it had stood for during its half-century: "*Country Life* likes to think that it has helped some decent things to be done in England, and that it has always set its face against deliberate commercial spoliation or … more ignorant vandalism in the countryside."

No one would have quibbled with that modest claim. Peace had come, but what was to be *Country Life*'s role in what Hussey had recognised would be a very different era? Set in the context of the grim austerity of the post-war years and the advent of the Socialist Welfare State, its very existence was a glaring anomaly. That it was to survive and flourish again was due less to internal than external factors.

The progressive social levelling which had destroyed the world which the magazine had celebrated was paradoxically to make that world — albeit in a different guise — accessible to more and more people as the ownership of motor cars and second homes spread through the middle classes.

In addition, the patriotic iconography enshrined in its pages was also to go unchallenged. Even the post-war Socialist government made no attempt to dislodge the potent images which had become part of national identity, deeply hierarchical and elitist though they were. The tableau of manor house, church, village, historic town and eternal landscape remained intact, awaiting their remorseless exploitation by the tourist industry which had yet to come.

These factors ensured *Country Life*'s survival, which was just as well since, for almost two decades after 1945, it cannot be described as anything other than worthy and dull. The fault for that cannot be laid wholly at the door of the nation's economic austerity.

Only after about 1960 is there any quickening of pace to what had

(Previous page) By 1963, the old London skyline had been eroded as the age of the high-rise block took its toll.

(Opposite) This poetic notion of England offers a curious juxtaposition to the reality of the post-war New Towns.

NEW TOWNS. By Sir Montague Barlow

COUNTRY LIFE

On Sale Friday
MAY 31, 1946

ONE SHILLING & SIXPENCE

IDEFORD VILLAGE, DEVON

A. Vincent Bibbings

become a virtual publishing dinosaur, whose contents week in and week out never changed and whose layout and graphic style, if they could even be called that, remained obstinately static. For the old established classes, the fact that it never changed must have given some sense of assurance and continuity in a world to which they increasingly could not relate.

The images and texts between the magazine's covers provided comfort to these classes, with its obligatory country house article, a garden, some sport, something on nature or the countryside, farming notes, book and exhibition reviews, safe female fashion for the county lady, pieces on antiques and answers to collectors' queries, a bridge column and a crossword. On the title page there still smiled an upper-class woman who would certainly have been presented at court.

Its contributors also seemed almost immortal. Christopher Hussey went on writing until he died in 1970. So did Arthur Oswald, who predeceased him by only a year. Major C. S. Jarvis, who began writing 'A Countryman's Notes' in 1938, continued writing up to the year of the coronation, 1953, and was succeeded by Ian Niall who only ceased contributing in 1989. Geoffrey Grigson and Richard Church dominated the book pages, Denys Sutton art exhibitions, G. Bernard Hughes antiques, A. G. L. Hellyer and Laning Roper gardens and, in 1958, Frank Davis began his saleroom articles which went on till he died in harness in 1990.

This gave the magazine an unrivalled sense of continuity and stability. New recruits only become visible in the early 1960s, with Michael Webb covering contemporary design, which had vanished from its pages for virtually two decades, and John Cornforth and Mark Girouard taking over as heirs of Hussey and Oswald.

Country Life is essentially a magazine which is looked at rather than read. If read during this period there emerges a striking gulf between the editorial page, which remained firmly in the real world, and the remainder of the magazine, where the overwhelming impression is of a composed image of an unchanging countryside.

The country house was celebrated in all its glory and the historic town remained a confection of Georgian streets. However, on the editorial pages country houses were either in crisis, abandoned or demolished, churches were being declared wholly redundant or in the grips of serious decay, old towns were raped as new roads were hacked through them or gradually ruined by developers, villages ceased to house country-dwellers and became instead dormitories for urban commuters, the rivers and seas were engulfed by pollution and the relentless suburbanisation of Britain forged ahead unchecked.

A grim picture which had much truth to it.

It is not until the middle of the 1960s, when a generation born into the new order of things took over, that *Country Life* finally accepted the inevitable changes in society. How isolated the magazine had become in the modern age was already evident in an editorial in September 1947, entitled 'In Defence of Quality':

> Space and order, dignity, elegance and grace, these are all snobbish, presumably because they have been associated with inequality (as all excellence, of its nature, must be) and Equality is the first of today's false gods ... The argument seems to be: We cannot all have the best, therefore no one should.

Country Life was clearly not yet at home in the new age of the common man. The magazine's role during these years was one campaigning for some damage limitation to the effects the new post-war society imposed on the cultural and visual infrastructure which had supported the previous status quo.

(Above) The thatcher's traditional tools.

A New Iron Age

If Britain was thought to be poor after 1918, it was in tatters after 1945 with a mountain of debt incurred by the war. In June 1949, Mr Attlee, the new Socialist Prime Minister, gave the prizes at the Architectural Association, promising young architects opportunities to design "fine public, industrial, and municipal buildings". A contemporary *Country Life* editorial is deeply revealing:

> … we have to peer very closely in order to discover the qualities of the national soul as expressed in architecture, realised or projected, under Mr. Attlee's Government so far … the truth is that the private patron in the past gave England a domestic architecture finer than any in the world. It yet remains to be seen whether Socialism can either build or design architecture as good.

Country-house building, which had continued up to the end of 1939 stopped. The magazine covered the few houses still being built, like Raymond Erith's Great House at Dedham, a Georgian essay in a modern idiom, and Basil Spence's Gribloch, Kippen, Stirling, "a notable expression of contemporary taste", but, it adds, "no country houses have been built for a decade". When, by a fluke, one was built in 1949-1950 to the designs of E. D. Jefferiss Matthews, its austere style was cited as a "vivid illustration of the social revolution of our time".

All the same, architecture was viewed by the magazine as being in the doldrums, its great tradition shattered. Hussey compared the new airport at Dublin unfavourably with the graceful harmonies of the Georgian city: "Much of the obscure sense of discomfort begotten by much modern architecture has been due to an apparent lack of a unit of design. Dimensions have appeared arbitrary and haphazard …" Seven years later, in 1954, there was a lament that "we have lost the old 'language of ornament' … and have not evolved a new one. Consequently few modern buldings are so designed that sculpture can grow out of them, and such of it as there is looks as though it had been stuck on afterwards." Much venom was expended on the Royal Fine Art Commmission (RFAC) as an "apathetic guardian of architectural standards in an era of conflict between material advantages, real or supposed, and those imponderable but eternal factors of taste and scale that reflect a civilisation's spirit". The end of building restrictions in 1955 brought no lifting of spirits, only a depressing litany of the implications of cheapness and the poverty of democratic taste:

> But when so many of our speculative builders of low-cost houses vie in pandering to sentiment and snobbery with the

(Opposite) The Coronation procession to Westminster Abbey, 6th June, 1953.

COUNTRY LIFE

Vol. CXIII   No. 2942

JUNE 6, 1953

THE CORONATION PROCESSION TO WESTMINSTER ABBEY PASSING UNDER A TRIUMPHAL ARCH IN THE MALL

'pseudo' — whether it is Tudor beams, Georgian trimmings, or jazz modernity — the Englishman's home becomes a peculiarly English horror which even kindly vegetation is slow to mitigate.

Looking back over the decade of 1945 to 1955, not a single building was thought by the magazine to be worthy of the ideals of the age. The Royal Festival Hall was deemed "negative" and Coventry Cathedral merely "original and colourful". Gratitude was expressed only for the survival of some good traditional rural housing and for well designed, wholly functional schools and factories. Once again, the Royal Fine Art Commission was castigated for being "less a stimulus to good design than an incentive to play safe".

As in the inter-war years, working-class housing was a major preoccupation, although unlike the earlier period, no pictures or discussion of the actual buildings ever appears in the main magazine. However, it returned relentlessly as a subject on the editorial page. Housing for the Socialist government meant only one thing — state housing. Private enterprise, and above all the landlord, were seen as the enemy. Rents remained pegged at 1939 levels, making it impossible for landlords to repair their properties economically. Subsidies for the modernisation of privately-owned rented accommodation were also withdrawn. In a bitter editorial in August 1946, *Country Life* attacked the government for its doctrinaire approach to a chronic post-war need and derided Aneurin Bevan, the minister responsible: "Better a State-built house sometime than one to-morrow built by somebody else who might be wicked enough to work for a profit". Bevan was guilty of presiding over a "doctrinaire administration based on an initial and glaringly false judgment ... wherever a comparison can be made between houses erected by private builders for profit and houses built by local authorities, the advantage of speed is always with private enterprise". Four years later, the magazine was still ranting on at Socialist prodigality "with its predisposition to ensure full employment rather than put the emphasis on efficiency, adventure and experiment".

The most innovative phenomenon of the post-war years was the New Town, an idea with origins in the Barlow Report of 1940, which recommended state action to decentralise the country's urban population, moving them out of the most congested areas and resettling them in new satellite towns. These, it was thought, would not only give those who migrated a better standard of housing but also provide areas of rural poverty with what they most needed — an injection of industry and population with a consequent increase in rates resulting in more funds available for the

(Below) The staircase at Gribloch, a 1930s fantasy worthy of the presence of Gertrude Lawrence.

(Above) Motor car ownership contributed to mounting pressure on the countryside.

improvement of local amenities. The New Towns Bill was passed in 1946, and fifteen such towns were planned. *Country Life* had previously featured a long series entitled 'Old Towns Revisited' — so long, in fact, that the practice of numbering each article was in the end abandoned. The reason why they were being revisited was made clear:

> So it is to these places … built by ourselves when younger and more sure of hand, that we should go for inspiration for our new towns, not to copy idioms of construction but to renew our faith in the possibilities of good buildings and architectural good manners.

Initially, there was no lack of faith in the new towns. In 1950, the magazine commented that they: "… constitute the outstanding contribution of our time to the physical aspects of Britain. In them … may well be found within the lifetime of many of us the creations in which coming generations will take most pride". What they called for most of all were the skills of the landscape architect in order "to create new towns in landscape, rather than landscape in new towns, more compact towns in real country".

Movement on them was, however, slow. By 1952, Hemel Hempstead had only a thousand houses and architectural ideals came up against the demands of the people who went to live in them. The architects wanted flats and terraces and three storey houses. The occupants demanded two storey ones, each with its own little garden. The result, where the latter were built, was therefore little more than a series of housing estates in a rural wilderness. They were devoid of any public buildings at their centre and devoid too of any sense of identity: "these ambitious and complex projects have been proving too costly in money, labour and materials under the conditions which have since developed". Disillusionment set in.

By 1959, the phenomenon of new towns was sufficiently manifest for judgement finally to be passed. Optimism that these would be the historic gems of the future had totally evaporated. They were condemned as being not even proper towns, but only over-large villages, their architecture dismissed as traditional and dull. They lacked any sense of community and, worst of all, the experiment had swallowed up untold thousands of acres of good agricultural land. Far from being new towns, they had ended up being dormitories for commuters to the large cities. No less than six hundred thousand people were trapped in these in the early 1960s, by which time they were "regarded by most of us and the architectural press", wrote Mark Girouard, "with (in many instances) a kind of cold-shouldering disapproving patronising despair".

With new towns written off as a disaster, attention turned to an alternative solution to the population bulge: the expansion of existing towns.

Proposals for this were viewed with extreme distaste by *Country Life*. The first was in 1953, when the London County Council agreed to build five thousand houses at Ashford, Kent, moving there not only the occupants but also the industry which supported them. The local authorities warmly welcomed the initiative. More houses meant more rates, and more people meant more customers for local retailers. The desecration of an old town was anathema to *Country Life*: "Development which is not natural growth is likely to alter considerably the character of the neighbourhood." The Town Development Act was passed the following year and included not only Ashford but Swindon and Bletchley. London now extended to a radius of seventy miles. Was this not, it was asked, "just a prelude to the suburbanisation of the whole of southern and south-eastern England?"

Much ink was also expended on the fate of London, whose devastation in the war had been seen as necessitating visionary rebuilding by an architect of the calibre of Lutyens. All this was to prove an illusion as the acres of grey bomb damage remained untouched for years. In 1947, Christopher Hussey reviewed the project for the City by C. H. Holden and W. G. Holford and found it "a soberly inspiring project", incorporating increased density levels of population by raising the building height and introducing bypasses and flyovers to mitigate traffic problems. In 1951, the London County Council Plan for London was shelved, as was a proposed ring road and instead Churchill endorsed the construction of a precinct around St Paul's which was to take up to twenty years to build. *Country Life* put in a plea that whatever was built should not be in the international style of the 1930s, which had led to "the same dreary, impersonal, urban conglomeration that could be anywhere", but in an architecture expressive of the British tradition, a combination of the romantic and experimental expressed through rational and classical proportions.

But, alas, this was not to be. By 1960, the developers had moved in as land values soared along with the buildings. The skyline of the City changed dramatically. In January 1962, the new buildings were condemned as "second rate" along with "the seemingly complete absence of civic design in their siting, which has permitted their concentration in areas both congested and historic on the old framework of corridor streets". The great American theorist on urbanism, Lewis Mumford, blamed the London County Council for turning London over "to investment for capital gains". This attitude to the transformation of the City was only to change in 1963 when the young Girouard could write more sympathetically:

> most modern office blocks in London are monumentally boring, but they are simple. Those interminable grids of glass and concrete have one great advantage … they act as excellent foils

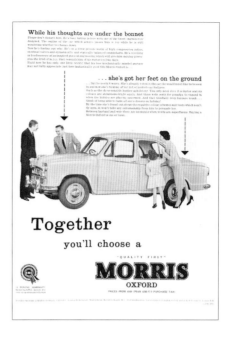

(Above) The family saloon arrived in the magazine during the early 1950s.

(Above) The Festival of Britain in 1951 epitomised everything with which Country Life *was uncomfortable.*

to buildings more worth looking at, or more elaborate in their detail … Experience seems to show that if you are going to have contrasts in scale, the bigger the contrast the better, usually, the result.

This woeful saga can be followed in the magazine's attitude to design which virtually disappears as a subject from its pages for over a decade, probably because what was happening was so at variance with its ideals of private patronage and traditional craftsmanship. The first blast came with the exhibition 'Britain Can Make It' at the Victoria & Albert Museum in 1946, which typified everything *Country Life* did not stand for:

> … the State has selected the things to be displayed rather than leaving the choice to the private patron … the consequence is that … preference is being given to the kind of things which people ought to like rather than those they liked in the past, or that they might like now if the circumstances were different.

The imposition of taste by "nanny State" was contrary to the magazine's principles and the editorial expressed its horror of "an exclusively mechanistic concept of planning and design" and called for "the re-establishment of human values".

Christopher Hussey went to the exhibition and recorded his revulsion in the hope that this "twenty-year-old vogue for the grimly functional has everywhere begun to look out of date ..." During the previous seven years, he had detected signs of a change of direction, stating: "... the last seven years, besides begetting a nostalgia for the past, have opened the eyes of idealists and realists alike to tradition as a source for some of the assurance and grace we are lacking today". Alas, nothing could have been further from the truth and his hopes were to be dashed.

This sense of tragic loss and misdirection also permeates Robert Lutyens' review of the Festival of Britain, that major manifestation of the ideals of the new Socialist utopia:

> Throughout, to the conventional eye, beauty in the old evocative sense can be lighted upon only in the old London across the river ... [The Festival] is a faithful reflection of a brave new world and, like it, difficult to make sense of in conventional terms ... the effect of the Exhibition as a whole is predominantly of contrasts amounting at first sight to discords ... Yet the very clash of shapes ... [has a] ... picturesqueness, though the reference is to contemporary abstractionism instead of romance.

(Left) An interior designed for the Council of Industrial Design in 1951. This picture was not published until as late as 1963.

This celebration of intellect and of the potentialities of science had produced an architecture "so spiritually lost ... that the spectator has the feeling on entering the Exhibition of going into a church without any holy place."

These years of austerity coincided with what amounted to a state patronage of modernism. *Country Life* turned its back on modernist design which did not return to its columns until 1963, when Michael Webb was brought in to write about it, but even then his first article was retrospective. The post-war years, he wrote, were ones of restrictions and lack of materials leading to crude standardisation. The Festival of Britain was "a false dawn" resulting only in "a rash of knobs, splayed legs, jazzy colours and patterns". Then came the influence of the Council of Industrial Design and the impact of Scandinavian imports which began to trigger a revival of interest in modern design. In 1956, the Design Centre opened in the Haymarket. Its products looked good but more often than not they failed to function properly. And it reflected "a lack of confidence in the nature of the modern movement — a feeling that it is somehow un-British", according to Hussey.

Elaine Denby's articles covered domestic artifacts, reiterating again and again the magazine's hostility to the modern movement, its austerity and standardisation. In her eyes, it ran counter to the established British tradition of mixing periods and styles. Apart from the kitchen and bathroom, where all things modern were now welcomed, the British were faced with a "challenging aesthetic". In January 1964, she wrote of the need to soften "unrelieved modernity", pointing the reader to the stylistic sobriety of the Regency and Georgian periods. The age of the decorator was about to begin. By the 1970s, John Fowler was to become the magazine's touchstone for interior design. His style, evolved under the aegis of the sybaritic American, Nancy Lancaster, matured during the post-war years. Fowler's country house interiors were to be recognised as the quintessence of English country house style.

If, in *Country Life*'s view, architecture and design were struggling through a new dark age, then gardening was too. The American garden consultant, Laning Roper, provided an overview in the *Country Life Annual* for 1962. The new towns, civic centres, factories and roads of post-war Britain, he wrote, all called for public landscaping on a large scale, but private gardening as known before 1939 was in retreat. Gardeners were becoming a thing of the past, and the great tradition of Lutyens and Jekyll was no more: "it would not be too wide of the mark to say that garden design has reached a new low". Gardens were reduced in size, their planting adapted to the limited resources of the new age. For the classes who read *Country Life*, these were the decades of defeat, retreat and a binding up of wounds.

(Opposite) Lady Anne Coke wearing a New Look dress with gloves to the elbow: debutantes such as her continued to be presented at court.

A Struggle to Survive

Austerity, social levelling, shortage of labour and materials — what possible future could there be for the great country houses? Week after week, they continued to appear in *Country Life*, still presented as seemingly untouched by the tide of the social revolution which surrounded them. In November 1945, the Marchioness of Exeter wrote the first in a series of articles on 'The Future of Great Country Houses'. She called for tax remission in respect of maintenance and repairs, the cost of heating and of curators to look after the contents. How could the houses ever even open without the help of staff? No one any longer wanted to be associated with something viewed as so ultimately demeaning as domestic service: "… it is the houses and their irreplaceable contents that require staff, not the personal needs of their owner-residents".

As Lord Methuen wrote in the article that followed, the government now at least recognised their significance. In the 1944 Town and Country Planning Act "for practically the first time the principle that the rich heritage of fine buildings should be preserved is quite clearly enumerated". In his concluding article, Christopher Hussey held up for emulation the decision of the French government to give 50% grants towards the upkeep of the great chateaux, and pleaded that in this country the government should similarly introduce tax allowances to enable houses to be open and for day-to-day maintenance.

But that was the last thing which a Socialist government could be seen to do in the post-war years — grant tax remission to those who were still regarded as a privileged caste living in splendour. In 1947, both Knole and Stourhead passed to the National Trust, giving rise to an embittered outburst by Hussey:

> The tradition, the handing down, of all this artistry is civilisation in tactile and visual form. It has been one of the services of those currently termed the privileged class, to whom, with strange absence of elementary good manners, it is the fashion not to say as much as a thank you when appropriating that which they have contributed to England …

In fact the Socialist government was to prove far less philistine to the cause of the great house than the Conservatives. Late in 1948, Stafford Cripps, Chancellor of Exchequer, appointed a committee under Sir Ernest Gowers to study the problem. *Country Life*, like the National Trust, reiterated its long held view that "the nation is the loser, when a great house ceases to be inhabited by the family whose continuity of tradition is its life …" The Trust offered "a palliating compromise" but one to be preferred to

(Opposite) A landmark: the first grants made by the newly created Historic Buildings Councils. Country Life *was later to become the major mouthpiece of the heritage lobby.*

THE FIRST HISTORIC BUILDING GRANTS

The first grants made by the Minister of Works on the recommendations of the Historic Buildings Councils comprise eleven for England, nine for Scotland and three for Wales. Some of the most notable but less known are illustrated on this page and the following one. Among English houses several are celebrated and scarcely call for illustration, for example, Lyme Hall, Cheshire (Corporation of Stockport), and Treasurer's House, York, (National Trust); also the Tudor gatehouse of Wolfeton House, Dorset, recently illustrated in COUNTRY LIFE. *Traquair House, Peeblesshire, and Craigston Castle, Aberdeenshire, are famous Scottish buildings. The reports of the Historic Buildings Councils, to be published shortly, will give an account of the initial months' working of the scheme. Meanwhile, these representative first-fruits, which together account for grants totalling £50,000, suggest that the Historic Buildings Fund is being at once wisely and economically distributed.*

(*Above, right*) THORNBURY CASTLE, GLOUCESTERSHIRE. Castle and early Tudor garden were begun by the Duke of Buckingham in 1511, but never completed owing to his execution in 1521. (Sir Algar Howard). (*Right*) DODDINGTON HALL, LINCOLNSHIRE. A notable Elizabethan house with gatehouse built in 1593 and fine Georgian interiors. (Mr. R. Jarvis). (*Below, left*) GAINSBOROUGH OLD HALL, LINCOLNSHIRE. The picturesque brick and timber quadrangle, dating from 1484, stands in Gainsborough town; the great hall is outstanding of its type. (Friends of Old Hall Association). (*Below, right*) WINTON HOUSE, EAST LOTHIAN. A masterpiece of Scottish Renaissance architecture, built for the Earl of Winton 1620-27, probably by William Wallace, architect of Heriot's Hospital, Edinburgh. (Mr. D. J. W. Ogilvy).

(Previous page) Bayons Manor, Lincolnshire, a great house abandoned and viewed from afar as a romantic ruin.

(Above) The curse of the car: buildings like these in the High Street at Tonbridge, Kent, were demolished for road-widening.

(Opposite) Before and after the Civic Trust: Thames Street, Windsor.

complete transfer to the state which only rendered such places "lifeless".

Gowers' Report — "the Country House Charter" — was published in 1950, and proved to be a landmark. It contained a mass of recommendations: no one should be penalised for living in such a property; a capital sum and the yield thereof needed for purposes of maintenance should be automatically exempt not only from death duties but ordinary tax and should be regarded by the state as being a fund held in trust. It went on to recommend the creation of two new bodies, Historic Buildings Councils for England and Wales and a separate one for Scotland. One of their initial tasks would be to list such houses and their contents. As the *Country Life* editorial on the Report concluded, much of it ran "counter to the present Government's ethics ... Yet the fairness and logic of the Report ... make it more likely to be implemented by a Socialist Government than by Conservatives, who would inevitably be charged with partiality".

A month later, the National Buildings Record published a list of nearly a dozen houses which had recently been demolished: "the well-meaning safeguards against indiscriminate destruction provided in existing legislation are at best negative, and generally useless, in enabling the preservation of what

156

1 and 2.—BEFORE AND (*below*) AFTER IN THAMES STREET, WINDSOR. About 75 street improvement schemes sponsored by the Civic Trust (an independent organisation founded in 1957, which relies for its resources on voluntary subscriptions) have now been completed; Windsor was the most ambitious project of 1961

should be preserved". Two years were to pass before the Gowers Report was partially implemented, and by then the government was Conservative. It had put the legislation, already in draft when Labour lost the election, into cold storage when Lord Chorley in the Lords pointed out the enormity of the situation. Of the four hundred houses listed by the National Trust for the Report as worthy of preservation, some forty had already gone and others were doomed. Those on a further list, which included Mapledurham, Holland House and Hill Hall, were "seemingly abandoned". In 1953, both Historic Buildings Councils were finally set up with an allocation for grants for repairs and maintenance. But tax remission to country house owners remained out of the question: "It is strangely illogical that the State should with one hand deprive their owners of the means of living in and maintaining them, and with the other grope for funds with which to repair them". But that was how it was to be.

Having jumped this hurdle, there followed the appalling sagas of the settlement for death duties of the Devonshire and Bedford estates. In the case of the former, Hardwick Hall passed out of possession of the family to the National Trust and major masterpieces from Chatsworth were transferred to the relevant national collections: "We may deplore the depths of ethics and economics that confiscate the goods of a family that during four centuries has been linked intimately with national history". The rape of Chatsworth was to be repeated with Woburn Abbey. Once again the magazine expressed its horror:

> As the resouces of heriditary owners and enthusiastic amateurs — the traditional custodians of secular culture — are levelled down, the responsibility of the nation is enlarged and in the near future looks like becoming absolute ... Where is the sense, let alone the logic or advantage, of a fiscal system that, unless more intelligent values prevail, may deprive both his and his countrymen of so historic, beneficent and irreplaceable a continuity as Woburn constitutes in our way of life?

There was, however, to be no let up over the toll taken by death duties but it was tacitly recognised that Chatsworth and Woburn Abbey had been mishandled. In the case of Ickworth and Petworth, the contents passed smoothly via the state into the custody of the National Trust: "the clause in the 1953 Finance Act relating to chattels is effective and valuable".

This was the period in which the privately-owned great houses began to open up in a major way. Penshurst, Hatfield, Chatsworth, Warwick Castle, Blenheim and Stoneleigh were already open by 1949. Longleat opened that year and Uppark, Nostell Priory and Wilton followed by 1951. Woburn opened in 1953 and, along with Longleat, was to set a very different style from its sedate peers, one which in the long run was more in tune with the demands of a democratic age. Everything from antique supermarkets to wildlife parks and the hosting of mass events brought in the crowds. The Duke of Bedford and Lord Bath, shortly to be followed by Lords Hertford and Montague, turned their estates into entertainment arenas. For all its dedication to the country house cause, not a whisper of this finds its way onto the staid pages of *Country Life*. One feels that such vulgarity was viewed as being *déclassé* and beyond the pale.

If country houses had become white elephants, churches were rapidly moving in that direction as congregation numbers began to plumet. From its very first pronouncement on the topic in 1949, *Country Life* was a staunch advocate of something the Church of England viewed with extreme reluctance as a last ditch resort: State aid. For a decade, no repairs had been carried out and churches were in an appalling state. By 1951, the Pilgrim Trust was so beleaguered by petitions for grants that it warned the Church that it could not go on paying for what should be the Church's own responsibility:

> It is no use shutting our eyes to the fact that, under the modern socialist system of wealth, all the parish churches that enshrine our history, if not still the creed, of our land will fall into decay if the people are not enabled to come to their rescue, or the State itself takes up the charge.

The following year, the Historic Churches Trust was launched and by 1956, alternative use was well under way with churches in Norwich being made into museums, libraries and a scout headquarters. But the problem was to accelerate. By 1958, three hundred churches were redundant; by 1960, another three hundred and seventy, with a further four hundred and twenty predicted to follow in the next two decades. The story of the fate of the parish church is there to be read in *Country Life*, but it never assumed the profile of either the great house or the historic town.

Towns, too, were struggling to retain their traditional character. The country's ancient towns were under attack from arbitrary expansion and from the increasing demands of the motor car. Chichester was mercifully spared since a ring road was built, as had been recommended by the magazine in its 'Old Towns Revisited' series. The proposals for Salisbury in 1949 eventually went through: "An unaltered medieval street is something so rare that every effort should be made to preserve it". Lyme Regis was to be another case about which Girouard was to write in 1960: "It is neither progressive nor realistic to widen a route that will never be suitable for modern traffic, and to ruin the town in the process." If roads were henceforth to be a permanent threat, so too by the early 1960s was redevelopment. By then

ARISTOCRACY REHOUSED

A FAMILY PORTRAIT IN THE NEW HOUSE AT LEUCHIE, EAST LOTHIAN.

land values had soared along with the population. C. S. Chettoe in May 1962 spelt out the horrors ahead in 'New Plans for Old Towns': the need for effective preservation orders, for bypasses instead of relief roads and the dangers of unscrupulous redevelopment. It was to be a cry in the wilderness. By the following year there was an anguished editorial:

> What went wrong? How is that, notwithstanding all the preparations for rebuilding cities intelligently after the war, little more than a decade has witnessed those high hopes end in architectural and traffic tragedy, principally through public inability to prevent private developers erecting high buildings out of place and out of scale?

The report of the Royal Fine Art Commission that year goes on to say: "It is not, we believe, at present realised what shocking schemes are afoot for mutilating some of the most beautiful historic towns — notably Bath, Salisbury and Cirencester — owing very largely to traffic flow over all other factors". This urban rape moved civic societies to join what was to become an unending battle.

The immediate post-war period witnessed a huge escalation in activity by the Bath Preservation Trust and the newly formed York Georgian Society and Regency Society of Brighton and Hove. In 1957, the Civic Trust was launched to play the role in towns once played by private patrons — to keep at bay the creeping universal suburbanisation and to rescue the inner environment from clutter, poor lighting and signage. A specimen street in Norwich was tidied up and repainted to demonstrate what could be achieved for only a modest outlay.

The problem, however, lay with the local authorities and the ineffectiveness of the post-war leglislation. The 1944 Town and Country Planning Act introduced the listing of historic buildings, and four years later, Building Preservation Orders came in whereby an authority could serve a notice prohibiting the demolition of a property for a period of two months in the hope of saving it. The inadequacy of this was soon apparent as owners deliberately allowed buildings they wished to demolish to decay. It was not until 1962 and the Local Authorities (Historic Buildings) Act that local authorities were empowered to make grants for restoration. Aimed at preserving modest urban vernacular architecture, it put a finger in the dyke to stem the tide of comprehensive redevelopment which was wiping out whole city centres.

The problem of preservation in London exceeded that in any other urban centre. It began with the fate of the Regent's Park Nash Terraces which, in 1946, were in an appalling state, shaken by bombs and often windowless, and only twenty of which were habitable. *Country Life* was sanguine about

(Above) A block of flats on the edge of Harlow New Town. Country Life *wrote: 'Tower blocks can add immensely to the variety and drama of the landscape', but by the 1960s disillusion with the New Towns had set in.*

THE ENGLISH ARCADIA

to their future: "perhaps, it might be possible to save and recondition one of the finest of the terraces — Chester or Cumberland, for preference … " A report under the aegis of Lord Gorrell the following year recommended their preservation, but nothing was done for a decade, during which they were patched up and used as government offices. Finally, in 1957, the Crown Commissioners decided to restore half of them and offer the remaining half to private developers. The magazine argued for the retention of York Gate, Chester and Cumberland Terraces, the rest being in its view "expendable". But they were all to be saved and restored thanks to the London County Council who, in 1962, refused the Crown Commissioners the right to demolish Sussex Place.

As far as London was concerned, the test case for preservation came with the proposal to demolish Thomas Colcutt's Imperial Institute in South Kensington to make way for Imperial College. Christopher Hussey's article, 'Save the Imperial Institute', raged against such barbarity:

> … the destruction of a great building, architecturally com-
> mensurate with the Law Courts or Westminster Cathedral,

(Above) The demolition of Imperial Institute, London in 1956, denounced by Christopher Hussey as an act of vandalism, was the great turning point in the rise of the preservation movement. It also led to the creation of the Victorian Society.

and its replacement by something unspecified, has been decreed by the Cabinet ... This cool resolve to erase the Empire's memorial to all that Queen Victoria's Jubilee stood for passes belief.

This was "a crime against the ethics of history and art" and the piece ends with a plea that at least its tower be saved, which indeed was to be the case.

But the crisis over Imperial Institute pushed things Victorian to the centre of the stage and there was to be a repetition of what had happened in the 1930s in respect of the assault on Georgian architecture. John Betjeman gave a lecture at Cambridge pleading for a more sympathetic assessment of buildings of the Victorian age, largely on literary and associational grounds, and in 1958, the Victorian Group emerged under the aegis of the Society for the Protection of Ancient Buildings.

Mark Girouard, who had only recently joined *Country Life*, was to become an important apostle for the movement as houses of that period, ironically in the styles the magazine had originally set out to disparage, were now accorded star status. The shift in attitude is caught neatly in 1958, when Girouard wrote pleading for the preservation of the Columbia Market at Bethnal Green which Sir John Summerson had categorised as "an encumbrance and a waste".

These were pioneering years for those dedicated to the Victorian cause and many battles were lost. In 1960, the London County Council registered no objection to the re-siting of the Doric Arch of Euston station and efforts to save its Great Hall failed. Two years later the City, "one of the least enlightened public authorities in the country", sanctioned the demolition of the Coal Exchange.

Mercifully, the government's proposal, announced in 1963, to demolish the Foreign and Home Office came to nothing: "a great unity of architecture and landscape, and so a supreme example of English art, has been condemned unheard to dismemberment".

Not only was the Victorian period reinstated in the aesthetic canon, but also a whole category of buildings and sites never before thought worthy of preservation — those which were the product of the Industrial Revolution.

In October 1959, there was the statement that "the selective preservation of historic industrial architecture demands the redefinition of the term 'natural beauty and historic interest' and corresponding reconsideration of the cost involved in it". Three years later, the Ministry of Public Buildings and Works initiated just such a survey.

Even taking into consideration what losses had already occurred, there was a sense that preservation had begun its long upward curve.

(Opposite) Brodsworth Hall, Yorkshire, one of the great Victorian houses which were re-discovered by the magazine during the 1960s.

The Pastoral Preserve

The condition of the countryside itself, facing a decimation to its acreage in the post-war era more lethal than that experienced even in the 1920s and 1930s, remained a growing concern for *Country Life*. On 13th August 1948, *Country Life* enunciated its view on the condition of the countryside in the age of the Welfare State:

> It is a commonplace now that most news is bad news. Those especially who care for the look of the countryside can scarcely open a newspaper without reading of a 'threat' to or 'spoliation' of some cherished part of Britain's landscape ... We may become too small, too poor, too imperilled an island to afford the luxury of aesthetic recreation. But we should recognise two facts. The first is that nationalisation of land is no remedy in itself. It is sheer hypocrisy in politicians to single out the private landowner — whose forebears have formed and protected the English landscape — as the main obstacle to the public's enjoyment of it. It is government departments that debar access; [they] have been the chief agents in the destruction of beauty ...

Country Life placed itself firmly on the side of the private landowner, against land nationalisation, and the increasing control of the countryside by the state and made a strong case for the role of the landscape architect. Immediately after the war, interest focused on the setting up of the National Parks, a move long supported by the magazine but which only came into being with the 1949 Act.

There was a profound unhappiness, however, as to how these parks were set up, for they were devoid of a strong central national authority — control of them was passing into the hands of the local authorities and the minister responsible. *Country Life* was never happy about these administrative arrangements, but its attention turned to the much broader issue of land use. "The past twenty-five years", it was written in October 1951, "have witnessed even more widespread destruction of Britain's rural scenery than that which took place when railways and industrialism blighted so much a century ago. Yet the self-destruction process remorselessly continues ..."

Unlike a century ago, however, people and powers were able to prevent the damage, but the country was faced with an ever-increasing rise in population and a concurrent need for housing. The National Farmers Union reckoned in 1953 that seven hundred and fifty thousand acres of farmland would be needed in the next twenty years for houses, schools, factories, airports and roads. The South East Study of 1964 was even gloomier: a

(Opposite) Fishing the Thame at Cuddesdon, Oxfordshire, in September 1963.

(Left) High Sunderland, near Selkirk, by
Peter Womersley, hailed as an 'outstanding
modern house'. During the 1960s a great effort
was made to cover what few country houses
were being built. This 'country house' was a
rectangular one-storey box.

growth in population of some three and a half million was estimated to take place in that area of the country by 1981, requiring not only the enlargement of existing new towns but of old ones as well.

Furthermore, *Country Life* realised the importance of new roads for the nation's economy and cast an envious eye towards the autobhans being built on the mainland of Europe. As early as 1948, it argued that the escalation in road traffic presented "a series of fascinating problems in combining its functional purpose with the preservation of the characteristic beauties of the landscape".

By 1959, there were seven million vehicles on the road and it was only then that the first motorways were built. They were too much the work of engineers and not enough of that of the landscape architect, the magazine commented, but it was crucial that they were carefully landscaped across the country and were not created by the widening of existing roads, thus wrecking towns and villages.

By the early 1960s, the lamentation over the ever-rising tide of traffic reached a crescendo. At the same time the break-up of the railway system began, cuttingmany a village off from its arterial network.

These changes meant that the countryside was a visibly different landscape by the early 1960s, since it had been subjected to two decades of incursion by a new society. To some, like the distinguished landscape architect, Sylvia Crowe, this alteration presented no problems, merely a readjustment of people's perception as to what was beautiful.

In an article entitled 'Power in the Landscape', she argued, amongst other things, that the lakes and dams called for by hydro-electric stations "can add beauty to the mountain landscape". Christopher Hussey in the same year, 1961, was to write his appraisal of the situation in a review of an exhibition jointly organised by the Arts Council and the Institute of Landscape Architects. Referring to his new-found hero, Lewis Mumford, he believed that whole regions must now be recognised as representing a humanised landscape, "the permanent green matrix of industrial life".

He reiterated his old mantra about the rape of the land during the nineteenth and early twentieth centuries, and stated that it was the precious heritage of the eighteenth century which offered salvation to the present

(Above) Road-building was to become a
major activity after the war leading to the
motorways of the 1960s.

problems, such as how to incorporate roads into the countryside. "It is to be hoped that ... the exhibition will have an exciting effect on the leisured population of the Welfare State". By then leisure had indeed ceased to be only the prerogative of the classes which in the past had created the countryside glorified by the magazine and now extended to embrace virtually the entire population. And that was to have profound effects, both positive and negative, in the coming decades.

In the midst of all this gloom, traditional values reigned perhaps in the only sphere where, up until then, it had been so signally absent: farming. Farmers were the only winners after 1945 when it came to the countryside. In 1947, the Socialist government passed the Agriculture Act, carrying out what the magazine had called for during the 1930s: state subsidy and the control of land use.

There was thus no return to the years of agricultural depression, only a continued drift from the land as rising wages forced farmers to mechanise more and more and to respond to the pressure put upon them by the government for higher food production.

168

As an editorial succintly put it in February 1952: "High farming is an essential part of Britain's defence programme…" Nor did the cessation of rationing lead to any changes in the policy of subsidy which, by 1959, ran to some £240 million.

Two events in the early 1960s, however, indicated that that golden age was drawing to a close. In May 1961, the Common Market raised its head, much to the dismay of the National Farmers Union: "… we cannot allow our agricultural policy to be decided by a Council of European Ministers sitting in Brussels or Strasbourg". With this in mind, in the same year, Sir William Slater, President of the Agricultural Section of the British Association, spoke out on the future of farming:

> British agriculture must either attempt to halt technical progress and rising output, relying on subsidies from the state for its future prosperity, or press forward ruthlessly, applying science to the full so that it can face fair competition without the need for Government support.

There was, in fact, he said, no choice. It was either go up that pathway or, minus state subsidy, re-live the pre-1939 depression. "Ruthless farming", as *Country Life* came to describe it, was to herald a new phase of life in the country in which those who lived there and those who worked there were no longer the same.

The battle lines were about to be drawn in Arcadia, where the very identity of the countryside itself would be under attack from powerful interests.

(Left) Time stands still: the Costwolds Hunt in 1959.

HERITAGE
1965-1985

The New Affluent Arcadians

The Heritage Cult

Arcadia Besieged

Creative Neglect

The New Affluent Arcadians

The austerity of the previous twenty years was to give way to a new affluence. In spite of the country's plight, progressively sinking lower in the economic pecking order, the massive expansion of the middle classes continued apace. The old upper classes, through increasing levels of taxation and an absence of servants, adapted to a far simpler style of living. They also began to enter professions and areas of endeavour which would previously have been looked down upon as "trade". The City had always been an acceptable place to work, as had government service, but now they embraced arenas like the sale rooms, catering, fashion, photography and the media. Simultaneously, there occurred the new generation of the meritocracy, the result of the Education Acts enabling those with talent to go to a university under the financial aegis of the state. By 1970, that generation was reaching its professional maturity and a vast majority of them made up the workforce of the new Welfare State as bureaucrats, doctors or university teachers. They were not only educated but affluent, with security of tenure, annual salary increases and a guaranteed pension on retirement.

These should have been the future constituency of the *Country Life* readership, but that was not to happen. The new affluence, which was such a notable feature of society by the middle of the 1960s, was expressed not only in the form of an ever-expanding market for consumer durables, but in areas which would also radically affect the countryside. By 1964, there were almost twenty million private vehicles on the road with predictions of twenty seven million by 1980. The upward curve of car ownership has always been accelerated by a government policy, regardless of whoever was in power, which has preferred road to rail transport. *Country Life* stood steadfastly, if rather forlornly, by the railways. The rise in car ownership meant that the countryside was invaded on an unprecedented scale, given the necessary roads. No longer were such incursions to be confined to the weekend, as holidays increased in duration until, for the upper echelons of the workforce, they could take up as much as a month or six weeks a year. "Leisure in the countryside", ran an editorial in 1972, "has become big business; what was predictable a decade ago is now with us; and the profits to be made from organising leisure for car-borne townsmen are likely to increase rapidly in the years ahead". People generally went to the countryside to take part in some kind of activity. By 1968, for instance, there were some three million anglers, and yachting facilities had multiplied by a factor of twenty during the previous two decades.

The mass exodus of motorised transport into the country developed into a semi-permanent invasion in the form of caravans and boats, and an

(Previous page) Stratton Park, Winchester, Hampshire. The original house, built by George Dance in 1801, was replaced by a new house which sheltered behind the portico.

(Opposite) A fashion plate from 1971 which glamourised the motor car.

THE ENGLISH ARCADIA

(Right) Holiday traffic in the Lake District in 1966.

increasingly permanent one in the form of second homes. Even by the early 1960s, the price of cottages located beyond the commuter belt — that is, a hundred to a hundred and fifty miles from the metropolis — had begun to spiral upwards. By 1973, *Country Life* could record: "Such is the demand for second homes now that there is scarcely an owner of a huge estate who is not pestered constantly to sell his old cottages".

What the magazine never chose to concentrate on was the change that this brought to the social structure of the countryside. The new country dwellers were urban and viewed the countryside in aesthetic terms fed by the very rural mythology which the magazine ceaselessly promoted. When they actually settled there, they found things were very different: blots on the landscape such as horrendous silos, vast sheds for battery hens and asbestos barns which, as farmers were exempt from planning restrictions, they were powerless to stop.

Even worse was the fact that many of the then usual normal farming practices repulsed them — like the mass spraying of crops with chemicals which wiped out wildlife, hedges and other animal habitats, the burning of stubble and the treatment of livestock as little more than objects fit for artificial insemination and tethering and destined to end up on a meat conveyor belt.

The new class of countryside dwellers changed the composition of rural society, but, like the indigenous landowners and farmers, these people were affluent and also articulate. They bore no relation to the class which was never referred to by *Country Life*, the depressed rural poor, largely inarticulate and in the employ of both the old and new affluent groups. Everything was set for a clash between the old and new country dwellers concerning the principles by which the countryside was to be governed, with the incomers embracing the growing environmentalist cause.

But why did these new aspiring classes adopt the rural ideal in the first place? In one sense, their embrace of it represented the victory of everything *Country Life* had stood for — the vision of England as a rural and bucolic environment. What was happening was that the lifestyle extolled by the magazine had been taken on in a diluted form by those who were socially upwardly-mobile. During the late 1960s and the early 1970s, a variety of circumstances outside the purview of the magazine served to escalate the cult of country living. The "flower-power" generation — young people aghast at the increasing materialism of the "You've never had it so good" society — opted out, creating for themselves a simple, homespun lifestyle in remote rural areas and eking out a living making pottery and growing organic produce. Then, in the aftermath of the 1973 oil crisis, came the

(Left) Caravans nestling in the grounds of Castle Howard, Yorkshire.

THE ENGLISH ARCADIA

years of bitter industrial unrest leading up to the 1979 "Winter of Discontent" which swept Mrs Thatcher to power. Strike followed strike. These hardly affected life in the countryside but paralysed life within the cities and towns as basic public services were disrupted, fuelling the increasing potency of the image of country living which was promulgated by such people as Laura Ashley, whose merchandise depended on settings depicting arcadian sunlit days peopled by pale-faced flaxen haired girls wandering through poppy-scattered cornfields. At the same time, interiors cultivated the country look with scrubbed pine furniture, flower-sprigged wallpaper, and the usual clutter of Victorian collectables mingled with the occasional product of the craft renaissance.

It is ironic that the Thatcher era did not dislodge this Arcadian myth, which became the aspiration of the boom years of yuppiedom. Fed by a glut of pre-1914 — and "upstairs-and-downstairs"-style films and television programmes, the country house ideal reached a new height in the public's consciousness. By 1990, even houses on council estates had festoon curtains at the windows.

The period from 1965 to 1985 was also witness to the increasing democratisation of this country's heritage, and the old patrician way of running historical institutions was obliged to take on the values of a more middle class constituency. Membership of the National Trust soared, along with visits to country houses and other historic sites: between 1972 and 1976, the Trust's membership doubled to five hundred and fifty thousand; by 1980 it had reached eight hundred and fifty thousand. Simultaneously, concern about the environment took off with the rise of the ecological movement. Paradoxically, all these were based on ideas originating from an urban consensus of what constituted the countryside.

What *Country Life* had encapsulated as an ideal in the early years of the century for a gently expanding middle class had, by the mid-1980s, exploded to embrace a large section of the population. But it was not to be *Country Life* which reaped the rewards of this tidal wave of adulation for all things ancient and rural. In fact, it was unable to respond to it, gripped as it was in a kind of mummification from which it was not released until 1987, when an outside editor was brought in to aid a magazine which was not only, as we shall see, in ideological crisis, but perhaps heading towards terminal decline. From 1965 to 1985, it was embalmed in a time capsule, in the same way as *Punch* and the *Illustrated London News* (the former was to fold, the latter is now only an annual), seemingly oblivious to what was happening in the world outside. All too often in this period, the magazine assumed the tone of a disapproving elderly aunt articulating the views of the landowner, the farmer, the members of the old upper classes with a

(Above) 'A selection of leafy, rosy papers found in nine out of ten English bedrooms': these patterns were typical of those advanced by designers in the 1970s.

(Opposite) The interest in heritage values had its impact on clothes design, as promoted by major designers such as Laura Ashley.

(Above) Dogs never left the magazine pages: 'Northcote Lucky Strike' won best show at Cheltenham in 1961.

place in the country and those concerned with heritage and the landscape — a miscellaneous patchwork of people drawn from the Lords and Commons, museums and endless quangos and societies involved in old buildings, the countryside and animals.

The look of the magazine was fixed as though in tablets of stone, its appearance virtually unchanged since the war. It refused to respond to the magazine revolution that had occurred in the previous decade. To look at a house covered by both *Country Life* and by *House and Garden* would leave the reader with the impression that he was looking at two completely different houses. While both magazines have different aims, the visual values of the latter could have offered a refreshing alternative to *Country Life's* approach.

In the former, the house's rooms remained devoid of life, empty and presented with an even tonality of light which was poles apart from the lush, lived-in look cultivated elswhere. Any notion that the magazine had relevance to readers below the age of forty vanished. The fashion pages alone are monuments to this stagnation.

There was certainly no attempt to accommodate the new middle classes, who were colonising the countryside and increasingly becoming its most vocal defenders. Consequently, different magazines — above all, *Country Living* — were to move in and cater for this new readership.

Other areas of publishing interest which *Country Life* had pioneered, such as antiques, architecture, interior decoration and gardens, were also taken over through the 1980s and into the early 1990s by new titles such as *The World of Interiors, Perspectives on Architecture* and *Gardens Illustrated.*

All of these areas, which would have moved the magazine on, remained undeveloped and if they were treated at all, were done so in an old-fashioned manner. The attitude *Country Life* exuded was sniffy, superior and progressively out of tune with the drift of the times.

When *Country Life* had started, it had pioneered much to do with the history of architecture and the decorative arts in this country — a distinguished achievement. But, by the 1970s, that scene had dramatically changed. Art history had become ever more professional and academic, with degrees in the subject at most universities and its own raft of journals. *Country Life* published works of original art historical research from time to time outside the country house articles, but they sat increasingly uneasily in the magazine.

The line between academic and non-academic publishing was being drawn ever-more sharply and the ability to straddle the two became more difficult to sustain.

That this happened is hardly surprising, for its famed continuity was now telling against it. When Geoffrey Grigson died in 1985, he had been reviewing for the magazine for twenty years. In the same year, its music critic, Stewart Deas, also died, aged eighty-one, and he too had been writing as far back as 1966. Amongst the younger generation, John Cornforth had joined the magazine in 1961, working closely with Christopher Hussey, and had become architectural editor in 1966. He was to remain with it for almost twenty-five years.

Many writers contributed for decades — Anne Price, the fashion editor, Ian Niall, who wrote 'Countryman's Notes', Frank Davis on the salerooms and Christopher Lloyd and Tony Venison on gardening. Lloyd indeed is still writing for *Country Life*. When a relatively young editor, Marcus Binney, aged only forty, was appointed in 1986, he did not receive the encouragement that perhaps he should have done to make the radical changes he wanted to give the magazine a new life and win a new and growing readership.

What staved off change was its continuing role as the prime agent for the sale of superior country property. It had the virtual monopoly of all the main estate agents and, with the property boom of the 1980s, these pages could be twice as long the magazine. As long as advertising revenue poured in, any pressure for change could be resisted as the magazine's old formula could be argued to be a continuing success.

These are judgements which can only be made by hindsight. Certainly no one who worked for the magazine — and often its contributors continued to be writers of distinction, like Marganita Laski — would have been aware of its increasingly isolationist position.

Many, if not most of them, during this period, are still alive and will certainly read these strictures with dismay but they have to be made. The successes of the conservationist and heritage bandwagon during these years, to which *Country Life* made a significant contribution, must have fuelled a belief that the magazine was more successful that it actually was.

As early as 1962, in an article entitled 'Towards a New Landscape', L. F. Gregory was to spell out the scenario for the countryside in the decades which lay ahead:

> The minority sees a process of spoliation … advancing across
> the working countryside, sweeping away traditional patterns
> and seriously disturbing the time-honoured image of rural
> England … This affectionate impression of rural England is,
> oddly enough, threatened by the very depths of its roots.

He continued: "The mid 20th century, however, wears a very different aspect. The wind of change has blown with mounting force. The Welfare State reigns supreme."

(Above) Supreme winner at Windsor and Leicester dog shows, 'Sealyham Alcide of Axe' was also 'an outstanding dog of 1961'.

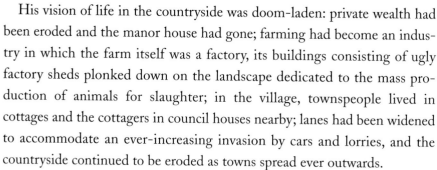

His vision of life in the countryside was doom-laden: private wealth had been eroded and the manor house had gone; farming had become an industry in which the farm itself was a factory, its buildings consisting of ugly factory sheds plonked down on the landscape dedicated to the mass production of animals for slaughter; in the village, townspeople lived in cottages and the cottagers in council houses nearby; lanes had been widened to accommodate an ever-increasing invasion by cars and lorries, and the countryside continued to be eroded as towns spread ever outwards.

More change, he predicted, was on the way. The eighteenth century had principles, this century none. We got, he concluded, the countryside we deserved, and nothing more.

The coming years were to bear his vision out. Already by the mid-1960s, hedges had begun to vanish, machines had moved in and an ocean of chemicals had been emptied onto the soil.

As early as November 1962, what were to become major environmental issues by the close of the century were signalled in an article by Frank Sykes entitled 'Does Modern Farming Menace Public Health'. This account of current practices told how chemicals used on seed-dressings led to the massive killing of game birds, rooks, pigeons and finches.

The use of artificial manure, phosphate, potash and nitrogen had already led to animal diseases and the use of sex hormones to promote animal growth "can have an effect on the consumer". Nonetheless, there was no alternative if the farmer was to produce cheap food.

In
hedg
the
whic
the
and
ence
blam
gove

N
the 1
had

In
"sup
leadi
farm

Reviewing the situation in 1967, Ian Moore wrote that the husbandman had now turned into both technologist and businessman in response to the furious rate of change due both to economic pressure and to the restrictive practices within the industry.

With the massive use of chemical fertilisers, the old rotation system was abandoned. Insecticides, fungicides and herbicides countered the ravages of pest, disease or weeds. New varieties of cereal were cultivated and new strains of livestock were bred in order to produce lean meat under factory conditions. In 1971, Charles Jervis wrote of "the strident cries of the food-faddists [which] seem too far from reality to be taken seriously".

The key 1960s publications which gave rise to the organic food movement — Rachel Carson's *Silent Spring* and Ruth Harrison's *Animal Machines: The New Factory Farming Industry* — were referred to, but there was a firm rejection that there was any evidence to support their claims. Instead, the magazine took a different view:

> the achievements of the scientist, particularly the chemist, in agriculture [which] in the last two decades have been astonish-

(Below) Ploughing a ley after treatment with the herbicide Paraquat, later condemned by the magazine.

who changed the landscape".

A year on, the question "Are farmers good guys or bad guys? ... destroyers of the countryside and its wildlife, despoiling the landscape for the sake of quick results" was coupled with an attack on the new campaigning organisation Friends of the Earth. All of this is vivid evidence of the magazine's view that its constituency lay firmly on the side of the existing landowners and farmers and not with the newcomers to the countryside. But by the middle of the 1980s, this was beginning to change, with the Common Agricultural Policy of the European Union which signalled the end of the government's cheap food policy and its long support for the farming industry. It was now left to market forces and the decrees of Brussels. *Country Life* recorded in October 1984 that "the time has come when agriculture should again be seen as the natural ally of conservation" and the following months recorded the close of an era in the history of the countryside leaving two options forward:

> ... either we continue with high-input farming on the present pattern, take some land out of production and attempt to devise ways mitigating the consequence; or we keep our farmed acreage at about its present level but change over to a new and modern system of farming with reduced outputs.

All the interested parties — the National Farmers Union, the Country Landowners Association, the Countryside Commission and the Nature Conservancy Council — were in agreement. The Common Agricultural Policy opened a door to reconcile conservation and farming in what was described in 1985, with the new Agriculture Act before Parliament, as:

> ... a total reversal of government policy, from encouraging farmers to produce as much food as possible, to persuading them to produce only as much food as is compatible with protecting the environment and restoring our depleted wildlife heritage.

In retrospect, the magazine's relentless support of the farming lobby regardless of much of its ecologically-insensitive approaches is perhaps the least reputable aspect of its history, and was a classic instance of the magazine failing to lead where it should have done.

Instead, it presented a calculatedly misleading vision of the rural condition during these decades. Those who gained most from these farming changes were those living in the urban centres whose need for cheap, easily available food was very real.

All the same, when they invaded the countryside, their attitude to what it represented was to prove both contradictory revealing of the ambivalent demands to which it was to be subject.

(Opposite) A field of barley at Little Maplestead, 1964, celebrating the huge increase in agricultural output thanks to 'ruthless farming'.

The Heritage Cult

Country Life had not started its life as a vehicle for the conservation lobby, but the 1970s witnessed a period when it was its prime journalistic organ for the conservation debate. It owed this pre-eminence to a succession of significant architectural writers and editors. Mark Girouard had pioneered the taste for and the preservation of Victorian buildings in the 1960s. He was succeeded by John Cornforth and Marcus Binney, both of whom were to be widely influential during the heritage crisis precipitated by the Socialist government's plan to introduce a wealth tax which loomed during the 1970s. Looking at the magazine's treatment of that crisis, it is striking how reluctant it was to portray the realities of this situation on its pages. *Country Life* had been built on and sustained by a dream: how could it cover its pages with grim pictures of demolished and crumbling country houses and churches, gardens gone to rack and ruin or rudely altered old towns? Although the battle was fought on the editorial pages, it rarely extended into the magazine in vivid pictorial form. This constriction certainly explains why Marcus Binney, in the aftermath of The Destruction of the Country House exhibition at the Victoria & Albert Museum in 1974, set up a campaigning organisation called SAVE, whose publications never held back from scathing attacks on central and local government and from printing dramatic visual evidence. It is probable that SAVE would have been unnecessary if the magazine had lived up to its ideals, but such stridency was viewed as being out of key.

By the mid-1970s, one word began to float to the surface of public concern with increasing regularity: heritage. By July 1978, comment was made as to how quickly this term had established itself in the public consciousness, but there is no doubt that the wealth tax proposals were largely instrumental. One catches it in the making in an editorial in April 1974, written in the aftermath of a budget which had increased the top rate of tax from 90% to 98%:

> The decision to despoil the rich will despoil their heritage of houses, parks and landscapes, but this is also the nation's heritage … the choice is between destruction and providing a situation in which owners can continue to carry out their responsibilities … It is the country as a whole that will pay the price for this destruction, which will be a sad end to Labour's traditional concern for preservation.

By adopting this train of thought, the opponents of the proposed wealth tax secured the high ground in the conservation for what, viewed dispassionately, was the preoccupation of only a very small minority of the

(Opposite) The end of a country house, Elmley Castle, Worcestershire: a tragic photograph taken in 1966. One of 780 such houses to be demolished in Britain since 1945.

CONSERVATION HEROES

MEMBERS OF THE CONSERVATION CORPS CLEARING CASSIOBURY PARK, HERTFORDSHIRE.

population. But theirs was an astute move, for they were able to present their cause as of universal concern, bestowing benefits on everyone and redressing the notion of private ownership into one focused on the stewardship of the nation's heritage.

1975 was European Architectural Heritage Year during which, it was noted, there was "a distinct swing in public and Government thinking away from the 'demolish and be damned' philosophy in favour of conservation and rehabilitation, [although it] has also been the year of one of our worst ever economic crises". Simultaneously, education began to come to the fore. Until 1970, there were still enough people around who could remember the old scheme of things. With the 1960s generation, deference to social class boundaries had entirely vanished, and appreciating the values and creations of a vanished hierarchical society now required information on the elements which had formerly made up its lifestyle, farming, gardens, historic buildings, wildlife and country houses. And this is precisely what happened as bodies like the National Trust and the Historic House Owners' Association took up the educational cause.

The 1970s were the heritage decade, and the birth of heritage as a universally-accepted concept revolved around the crisis affecting the country house. In August 1973, John Cornforth summed up the change of situation as follows:

> A few years after the war there was a recovery that probably no one could have envisaged in 1945, and this continued until 1965 when the capital gains tax was introduced. Now, as we approach the mid 1970s, the prospects for the future are much less optimistic, and indeed in many cases extremely gloomy …

The problem had already emerged briefly in 1969, when the future of Heveningham Hall was in question. In that case, the government stepped in and purchased it. By 1973, Cornforth was already engaged in writing his important report on the future of country houses under the aegis of the newly set-up Historic House Owners Association. But again it was the wealth tax proposals which triggered a mighty crusade on behalf of the country house.

There was a huge surge of activity throughout that year aimed at gaining exemption from the wealth tax of objects also exempted from estate duty. In July, the tax was seen as undoing everything which had been achieved since the war and, for the first time, the magazine tossed a bouquet to those pioneering country house owners whom, until then, it had viewed with condescension and whose activities it had deliberately ignored: "the attitude which condemned the owners of Woburn and Beaulieu for commercialism must be cast aside". Proposals for the tax were "based on a hostility towards private inherited wealth" and, as such, represented an unprecedented danger to the survival of country houses, gardens and landscape parks: "Even if a system for protecting this aspect of the Heritage is worked out, the Capital Transfer Tax, combined with removal of agricultural abatement, is bound to destroy its economic foundations".

By the autumn, the campaign in defence of the country house reached a crescendo with the publication of Cornforth's *Country Houses in Britain. Can They Survive?* and, in the autumn of the next year, the Victoria & Albert Museum's exhibition: "We face not only an attack on a central part of our artistic patrimony, but the most serious assult on the face of the countryside since the Industrial Revolution", ran an editorial on 3rd October, somewhat over-stating the case. But the magazine rose from its inertia to play a crucial role in a campaigning network which ran through the media and the art world to secure the provisions which were embodied in the 1976 Finance Act. By then, the government had abandoned the wealth tax as it could not cope with a major flood of country houses going under. It was realised that as far as the state was concerned, it was cheaper to leave houses in the hands of their owners with some fiscal concession to enable them to survive. The 1976 Finance Act was hailed as a landmark:

> Government's acceptance of the principle of maintenance
> funds for historic houses could mean that the 1976 Finance
> Act will be remembered as a milestone in the history of British
> preservation ... it will ... go a long way towards providing a
> future for a large section of the national heritage and do much
> to restore vital confidence and incentive.

That year saw the sale of the contents of the Rosebery house, Mentmore, which seemed to belie this optimism, as the government decided not to acquire it in January 1977. By the close of the 1970s the climate for country houses had radically changed. A huge shift in public opinion had been achieved in which the magazine had played an honourable part and the country house cult enjoyed by middle class culture entered its 1980s heyday. In 1980, the magazine recorded with pride that, since 1974, a hundred and twenty outstanding country houses had been offered for sale in its pages. The only "losses", if such they could be described, were Warwick Castle and Mentmore. The crisis had triggered the events which led up to the recasting in 1980 of the old Land Fund as the National Heritage Memorial Fund, which enabled deals to be done saving houses like Canons Ashby, Calke Abbey and Belton House for the magazine's old ally, the National Trust.

Country houses were not the only buildings under threat. Churches also rose to the top of the agenda in the 1970s. They appeared in the magazine as if by stealth, for *Country Life* had always avoided being churchy, although

A SENSE OF DIRECTION

THE QUANTOCKS TO THE BRENDON HILLS: STUDENTS ON A 'MAN IN THE LANDSCAPE COURSE'.

its commitment to state aid never wavered. Under Archbishop Ramsay, the shift in that direction began. "After a gallant struggle for nearly 60 years against ever-increasing odds", ran an editorial in September 1971, "some aid from national resources has become a necessity in all parts of the kingdom, if these visual symbols of history and national character are to survive". But nothing was forthcoming for a church increasingly beleaguered by declining congregations, roaring inflation and by the imposition of VAT on repairs.

It was only in the aftermath of the Victoria & Albert Museum's Change and Decay: The Future of Our Churches exhibition in 1977 (for which the magazine's Marcus Binney was largely responsible) that government implemented grants of up to £1 million via the Historic Buildings Council. But churches were only peripheral to the magazine's heritage concerns.

Far closer to the magazine's interest was the fate of historic towns. Michael Wright, the magazine's editor during this period, wrote about the town of Banbury and spelt out what was true of all the historic towns when he lamented the "dull uniformity by modern commercial presentation, large display windows and standard fascia boards". Houses were turned into shops, their upper floors left empty, thus eroding population from town centres. Articles spelt out the fate of these towns as, hungry for financial rewards, they took in thousands of Londoners and created new industrial estates on their perimeters. The towns which fared worst were those within reach of the London commuter belt: in Bedford, located at the end of the commuter line from St Pancras, the population went up by a quarter between 1959 and 1965, causing indiscriminate expansion and the destruction of much of the town's centre.

The tide only slowly changed when the 1972 Local Government Act gave the new planning authorities powers to control the demolition of buildings within a conservation area even when they were not listed. Much to the approval of *Country Life*, the Historic Buildings Council was empowered for the first time to make grants on a 50% basis of the total conservation costs.

As a result, the tide of destruction began to be stemmed in cities like York and Chester, but it was to depend always on the commitment of the new local authority. Where this commitment existed, the results can be seen today in cities like Norwich. Where it was absent, the aura of desolation remained and was to be accelerated in the 1980s as out-of-town shopping contributed further to inner city decline, leading to the present "doughnut" effect. But that story was largely unchronicled by the magazine which showed little commitment to the urban cause during the 1980s, when Thatcherite economics began to take their toll.

(Previous page) Mavisbank, Midlothian: attempts to acquire the fine William Adam house on compulsory purchase failed. It is still a ruin today.

(Opposite) The decaying church at Great Livermere, Suffolk, which featured in the 'Change and Decay' exhibition at the Victoria & Albert Museum in 1977.

Arcadia Besieged

In January 1978, *Country Life* reiterated its position in respect of what should happen to the countryside:

> For the past twenty-five years *Country Life* has been proclaiming the doctrine that Britain needs a land-use policy … we have squandered the asset as though we had an inexhaustible supply, and could afford to bring even the best of it under roads, airfields, factories and houses.

This principle reflected the expectations of its readers, for it has to be admitted that the sacrifice of large tracts of the countryside for the purposes of new factories, towns and transport networks brought for the majority of the population what they most desired — a house of their own with a garden, cheap factory-produced consumer goods, the ability to travel by car and employment.

Consumer affluence has dramatically increased pressure on the countryside. The conversion, in 1965, of the former National Parks Commission into the new Countryside Commission for England and Wales was welcomed as a means of coping with the onrush:

> … a series of Country Parks, where picknickers can enjoy the countryside, to be created by the local authorities with Treasury assistance; the planned growth of recreational facilities on reservoirs and canals; more camping and caravan sites, and additional long-distance foot paths; amendments to the traffic regulations affecting national parks … a substantial programmeof tree-planting by local authorities to enhance the landscape — all these measures should help to harmonise growing demands with the needs of the countryside.

Writing in April 1966, Garth Christian's article is headed 'The Countryside under Invasion': by then half a million people went sailing, one and a half million camping. Before 1939, eighty thousand people made use of the Norfolk Broads, but now it was three hundred thousand. There was one saving grace in what could become a tide of destruction: "Increasing use of the countryside by the people of the towns could eventually arouse a national sense of concern for its conservation". The theme of how to reconcile access with preservation was to become an ever-recurring concern. When the Countryside Act and its concomitant Commission came into operation in 1968, it was welcomed. So too was the creation of the Department of the Environment the following year which, for the first time, brought all land use under the control of one ministry able to cope with the problem posed by escalating pollution and leisure and the demands

(Opposite) Ramsgate Harbour and yacht moorings, on the Kent coast, which was the focus of an article citing the pressures of tourism.

THE ENGLISH ARCADIA

THE M23 / M25 INTERCHANGE

'WHAT OUR PLANNERS CAN DO TO THE COUNTRYSIDE WHEN THEY REALLY GIVE THEIR MINDS TO IT'.

arising from entry into the EEC.

Conservation steadily dominated the agenda through the 1970s with the Wild Flower Protection Act (1973); recognition of the consequences of the loss of the landscape parks ("the time has come to give urgent consideration to the fate of those that survive" wrote Binney in 1974); and endless battles over the siting of new airports. By 1976, even the Department of the Environment put preservation ahead of public use in the case of the National Parks. Dutch elm disease and the depredations of ruthless farming led to the launching of National Tree Week in 1977.

If the countryside was invaded by the public, it was eroded more seriously by central and local government as its land was swallowed for roads, factories and housing. The magazine's policy on roads was enunciated in an editorial in August 1976: "It has long been the view of *Country Life* … that road transport far from being the communications medium of the future, is already obsolescent, because it is inherently labour-intensive and wasteful in land-use." The magazine's attitude to transport railed against cars and more roads, favouring instead public transport, especially the railways. Ten years previously, Brian Dunning, writing in the aftermath of a decade of M-motorway construction of which, by 1970, there would be some thousand miles, stated: "Not since the days of the enclosures has our landscape been subject to such a swift and permanent change." In the same way that the enclosures had created the landscape from the eighteenth century, so these new roads restructured the country in the twentieth century, acting as rivers which could divide as sharply as they could unite the points of the compass they linked. "The motor car, unless we can somehow control the flow, will inevitably engulf our own countryside."

But nothing was to counter the flow of cars which continued to soar ever upwards and which, after Britain joined the EEC, was increased by the advent of the juggernaut — providing another topic for editorial breast-beating. *Country Life* never had a good word to say in favour of successive governments' road policy which they viewed as the destroyer of essential food-producing agricultural land and the cause for the despoliation of the countryside.

Worst of all was the impact of the new roads on historic towns with demands for road widening, parking facilities and ring roads. The devastation caused by traffic was a key factor behind Richard Crosland's Ministry of Housing and Local Government's Commission in 1966 to study the problems of four towns: York, Chichester, Bath and Chester. The first to appear was the report on York in 1969, which recommended the removal of all through traffic except that which was residential, a policy which was implemented in the mid-1970s with the introduction of pedestrianisation.

The 1970s and 1980s were the decades of the bypass, which attracted the magazine's enthusiastic support, although the Civic Trust by 1983 was doubting whether they did in fact offer a solution: "it has long been the view of *Country Life* that the only answer is to adopt the pattern of our continental neighbours and carry more freight by water and by rail". But they were a voice crying in the wilderness.

By the mid-1980s, the green belt around London was being used for the new M25. The green belt was a sacred cow for the magazine, and its existence was never questioned even though in reality it often protected land of no great interest and it arguably only exported urban sprawl even further.

The village still appeared on many a nostalgic cover, but in the 1970s its decline became a major topic for concern. In July 1978, an editorial ran: "The deserted village of the 1970s is a more alarming problem than it was in Goldsmith's day because of all the other pressures that threaten to destroy the stability of English social life." Villages required families and adequate public services. In the 1980s, a degree of small business endeavour offered some hope but more often than not it was the village shop and post offices which disappeared.

Much ink was spent eulogising the vanishing village, but villages had long ceased to have economic value as farms required fewer workers and the middle classes moved into the houses, creating other sorts of changes: "Once simple houses now suffer from every mistake in the design book and this could get worse …", wrote John Cornforth in aesthetic horror. The magazine now preoccupied itself with issues such as urban infilling, car parking, signage, advertisements, DIY front doors and the wrong kind of fenestration.

What was not mentioned was the fact that there was still an indigenous rural population living in council houses and working for low wages and, as Thatcherism bit deeper, experiencing a contraction of Welfare State services and the withdrawal of public transport.

Pollution, however, rather than poverty, was to become an obsessive subject from the 1970s onwards. Although the government announced a programme to clean rivers and estuaries, not much headway was made even by the 1980s. In 1973, dieldrin and aldrin were withdrawn, having killed off many species of wild birds, but it had already been washed out to sea. By the mid-1980s, the environmental lobby, although divided, had become powerful and was being consulted by government.

All the same, words like "national" and "heritage" were thrown around easily by those in government and in the press, even though the practical effects of presentation campaigns were rarely realised to their full potential.

CONFLICT IN THE CITY

THE URBAN LANDSCAPE WAS ALSO SUBJECT TO MASSIVE INCURSIONS BY MOTORWAY FLYOVERS.

Creative Neglect

After 1945, *Country Life* was never very happy with contemporary creativity. One will look in vain for the elements which gave the magazine such verve between the wars, ones which dealt with the updating of country houses to modern standards or with contemporary craft, especially interior decoration. Music, theatre, ballet and exhibitions of conventional art were reviewed, but the nearest the magazine got to contemporary creativity was its annual visit to the Royal Academy Summer Exhibition. Design, which had been one of its key themes through the inter-war years, vanished. These omissions all reinforced its reactionary image, embodying the visual taste of "Disgusted of Tunbrige Wells". As a magazine essentially read by the establishment classes, a great opportunity was missed to encourage them to develop.

It is striking that even in its architectural coverage *Country Life* drew back, abandoning its role as the architectural conscience of the nation. By the mid-1970s, the subject was dropped and one looks in vain for comments on key works by Foster, Rogers and Stirling. Articles on new architecture had limped on through the 1960s, in the main under the aegis of Mark Girouard and Michael Webb. Domestic architecture just slipped away. James Gowan's house in Hampstead in 1965 was the last appearance of a temple to modern gadgetry and new affluence. But there were to be no successors. In 1968, Christopher Hussey criticised a small modern bungalow on the Sussex coast for its negative qualities. In his old age, everything was to be subservient to the landscape: "it will be increasingly necessary to evolve architectural means for merging adjacent or permissable structures inconspicuously into the landscape, yet without prejudicing such buildings' aesthetic integrity as architecture".

Architecture when it did appear focused on certain public projects, like the new regional theatres. In 1964, the magazine asked why current buildings were so dull, apportioning blame on the clients who did not know what they wanted and who inevitably opted for the cheapest materials. The planning system "tends not only to operate against good design but to put a premium on bad …" Frederick Gibberd's Roman Catholic Cathedral at Liverpool was praised for its interior "encased and manipulated by light" but "little of the art is distinguished" and the external altar was unsuccessful. So too, it was judged, were the expensive additons to Oxbridge colleges. Unsurprisingly, no sympathy was shown for the "new brutalism" of the Hayward Gallery on the South Bank, only utter dismay at its "disharmony of proportion … the vistas bare or congested". Later, in 1968, Michael Webb went on to condemn the whole lifeless South Bank as a "concrete

jungle through which few explorers pass". All of this reflected a deep unhappiness about the eclipse of private practice and the rise of the local authority architect. In 1974, there was at last a full-frontal attack: "few can doubt that architects in Britain today face a loss of public esteem, confidence and even trust, second only to that which confronts developers and planners". The conviction of the modernist movement that "a new architecture could solve the ills of the world" had failed. And with that, contemporary architecture vanished from the pages of the magazine for a decade.

And so architecture was not to the magazine's taste and country houses were no longer being built. The latter were, however, being redecorated on a scale unseen since before 1939. It is quite astonishing that the magazine ignored what could have been a subject richly appropriate to its readership. The work of David Mlinaric and David Hicks, both concerned with making old country houses work in a contemporary context, was not featured. Both did much of their finest work during this period when interior decoration was undergoing a renaissance, transforming country house interiors. Indeed, the English country house interior by the 1980s was to become an international style exported all around the globe. One will look in vain in the pages of *Country Life* to find any reflection of this. Decorators were looked down upon and it was not until Cornforth "discovered" John Fowler in old age that their presence was allowed in the magazine's pages. Gloom about the present also featured in the garden pages. In 1976, Tony Venison, the magazine's gardening editor, wrote on 'The Problems of Large Gardens'. By then anything above about half an acre was considered to be large. A litany of threats was listed: rising costs, the lack of skilled labour, changes in land values and usage and, more than anything, the fact that private ownership was under fire. There was also roaring inflation. All contributed to a doom-laden atmosphere. The most important gardens would survive, government being able to make grants for their upkeep, but otherwise the outlook was "bleak".

By the middle of the 1980s, *Country Life* was becoming yearly more peripheral as it trundled out ideals and attitudes which had had vibrancy earlier in the century, but which had already lost much of their energy by 1939. Just as 1945 was a dividing line in social reform, so 1979 was to be an even stronger one. The old upper class viewpoint sustained by *Country Life* still had some hold in the Conservative party and in the shires, but Thatcher epitomised the triumph of Middle England. This finally rang down the curtain on any lingerings of the old world of *noblesse oblige* and aristocratic cultural hegemony. The age of market forces had arrived. Perceptions of the nation's rural identity moved away from the old Tory

(Opposite) A kitchen designed by James Gowan for a house in Hampstead, London, in 1965. Its clean lines still seem modern today.

(Above) The South Bank Centre, London: 'it is desirable to attract those who are not already arts-minded' wrote the magazine in 1968.

Baldwinesque vision of a gentrified Georgian England to one focused on service industries, business parks and the City. As far as prime ministers were concerned, Chequers was a conference centre and not a country house. The aristocracy finally went to the wall in favour of thrusting businessmen who now were advanced to all the key positions.

As a magazine, *Country Life* was being undermined not only by competitors but also by intellectual challenges. The attack from the left was sharply summarised in an article by the Chief Strategic Planner for the Greater London Council, David Eversley, who in 1974 wrote an article in the *Built Environment Quarterly* entitled 'Conservation for the Minority?' It is such a scathing attack on the world to which *Country Life* and the other organs of the preservation-heritage lobby belonged, that it should be quoted in full:

> A tiny minority of self-appointed arbiters of taste dictates what the living standards of the rest of us shall be ... One rapid glance at the composition of the official bodies which can prevent any change by their edicts, the unofficial pressure groups which back them, the leading individual writers who monopolise the subject in the press, all show us who they are: the ever-present establishment, the landed aristocracy, the products of Oxford and Cambridge, the landowners, the officer class, and, behind them, their hangers-on: the trendy academics with less pretensions to gentility who prove their club-worthiness by espousing their elitist views ... They are continually mourning for a past where they, and they alone, had a right to tranquillity, the open countryside, distant coasts, spacious surroundings, plentiful and humble servants, and were in receipt of the safety and convenience provided by public expenditure. They loathe an extension of these privileges to the majority of the people.

One million acres of *land* might have been lost since the last war, but between 1945 and 1975 1.5 million people as a result have a *home* of their own. Embittered though Eversley's viewpoint might have sounded, it was one which deserved answering.

What might be called the attack from the right came in the 1980s, when academics began to analyse the socio-political background which prompted not only the launching of *Country Life* but the whole heritage cult and its symbiotic relationship to notions of Englishness.

Of these the most important was Martin Wiener's *English Culture and the Decline of the Industrial Spirit 1850-1980*, which appeared at the opening of the Thatcher decade. The book traced how the attributes which had created the Victorian entrepreneur — hard work, money-making, inventiveness and a driving zeal for production — had been discarded in favour of those seen as appropriate to the gentleman, the cultivation of style and the pursuit of leisure, along with those of political service. This change of values resulted in the rejection of the positive aspects of an urbanised society in favour of a cultural ideal which was rural, epitomised in the country house, the shoot and the garden.

These were the very ideas which underpinned *Country Life*, and Wiener's book went on to argue that this had been a contributory cause for the country's loss of economic dominance, criticising Britain's innate conservatism and caution, instead of those virtues which had once made it a world leader, a passion for change and for everything that was new in technology.

The magazine dismissed the Wiener book brusquely in an editorial, but its charges cannot so easily be brushed aside, nor those of Eversley. Ideas take time to percolate but both criticisms lit fuses which in the long term could have had a fatal effect on the future of *Country Life* unless changes were made. This is precisely what began to happen after 1986, much to the consternation of the old guard.

(Below) Falmer House, the University of Sussex: 'the buildings convey an air of quality, of modernity blended with traditional dignity, of an expensive experiment'.

LANDSCAPE
1985-1997

New Lamps for Old?

A Classical Revival

A Crowded Landscape

New Lamps for Old?

By the middle of the 1980s, *Country Life* could either have continued catering for a diminishing elite or taken a leap into the future. By then it was one of a raft of magazines published under the aegis of IPC Magazines Limited, and housed within King's Reach Tower, a high-rise block south of the river. The great days of a Lutyens building in Tavistock Street had long since gone. It was now just one among many upmarket magazines which had to pay its way in a fiercely competitive marketplace. With all the pressures that such a commercial conglomerate might have imposed on any of its magazines, it is surprising that *Country Life* should for so long have gone unchanged.

But, in the late autumn of 1986, an editor from one of IPC's other publications, Jenny Greene, was made editor. She was succeeded in 1993 by Clive Aslet. It was during this last decade that *Country Life* underwent the greatest transformation to both its appearance and contents since its foundation, one not welcomed by all its readers, for whom the recent changes were seen as desecrations of a minor national monument.

By the end of 1988, *Country Life* was a different publication. There were colour illustrations throughout most of its pages and its typography and layout changed (it still is changing). Human activity in the countryside was featured for the first time for decades and issues were tightly themed. Rooms in country houses even sported the odd lived-in touch, like a stack of books on a table or desk, something which would once have been quite unthinkable. The fashion section included clothes which could be worn by people below forty and even men's fashion began to feature. Garden plans were introduced. Film and television were reviewed for the first time.

The old contributors were phased out one by one, for the vitality of any magazine in the late twentieth century does not depend on fixtures. Ian Niall, who had written for the magazine since 1950, lost his monopoly on 'A Week in the Country' in 1989. The following year Frank Davis, who had covered the salerooms since 1957, died in harness in his late nineties, and a whole group of younger writers was brought in, bringing a breath of fresh air to the stale pot-pourri.

The economic boom in the 1980s saw the magazine reaching a new generation of readers in much the same way as it had at the end of the last century when, under the shrewd hand of Edward Hudson, it aimed at those with new money. The more recent wave of prosperous country dwellers was described in an article on houses and commuting in January 1989:

> … a new technological squirearchy has beaten time and distance into the country property market. Computer-linked at

(Previous page) Stainforth Bridge, Yorkshire Dales, a picture reflecting the 1990s 'greening' of Country Life.

(Opposite) The Georgian summerhouse at Dalmain, Cumbria. The introduction of softer and more romantic covers attracted a new female readership to the magazine.

THE ENGLISH ARCADIA

COUNTRY LIFE

AUGUST 18, 1988 £1.20

home, in contact by mobile telephone and fax while on the move, this new generation of country house buyers is no longer restricted by travel-to-work time, and is able to operate from a rectory in the Welsh border country as from a town house in Holland Park.

In describing this new social phenomenon, the author dismisses it as largely a myth. But there was truth in it. The change in the social composition of those living in the country derived from the explosion of property values in the mid-1980s, when people realised they could purchase a far better house in the country than in central London. The property pages of the magazine now numbered well over two hundred. This was the first time since the turn of the century that the well-off did not feel under threat from punitive taxation. In 1989, the top rate of tax was 40%; a decade before, it had been 98%.

These were boom years, in which new fortunes were made from electronics, financial services, advertising and retailing. But while this money was made chiefly in the cities, landownership was still a large issue. In February 1989, James Scott recorded how Britain still remained the "only country in the world where the ownership of rural property confers status".

Although in the same issue it was noted that from 1978 to 1988 two hundred and fifty traditional family estates or principal residences had been sold, 10% of an overall total, there was no lack of buyers for them. The changed economic climate of the period "allows the newly rich to treat their estates as an oversized garden rather than as a business, much as they would 100 years ago".

The issues of the magazine before the collapse of the property market and the recession are a unique phenomenon in its post-war history. They exude a technicolour opulence which forms a vivid contrast to the strained quality of those issues dating from the mid-1990s when they dramatically shrank in size.

In the late 1980s, the magazine reeked of that decade's consumerist ethos and wallowed in the attainment of the supposed accroutrements of taste rather than in discriminating taste itself. The advertisement pages are an index of conspicuous consumption on a gigantic scale, embracing Gothic conservatories, garden temples, period wall-papers, interior decoration and courses on antiques.

Even although this boom was to fall off dramatically with the onset of recession and the collapse of Lloyds, not since before 1939 had there been such a surge of activity in building, interior decorating and garden-making, a rising tide of confidence which was to find its architectural expression in a new interest in things Classical.

(Above) The typical 1980s middle-class couple, with a house in the country, from a 1988 issue.

(Opposite) Danes Cottage, Surrey, 1981. Typical of the smaller gardens covered in the 1980s.

A Classical Revival

In October 1984, after an absence of almost a decade, the subject of contemporary architecture returned to the pages of *Country Life* with an evangelical fervour, unseen since its advocacy of Lutyens earlier in the century. It was generated by interest in two architectural causes: that of the post-Modernists and that of the new Classicists. The latter were in fact continuing the traditions of the old classicists, for the building of elegant small country houses in the classical style had quietly gone on since 1945, but it was hardly referred to by the magazine.

Interest in this forgotten phase began with a series on the Yorkshire-based architect Francis Johnson, who had designed classical houses in the 1960s. The work of Raymond Erith was also rediscovered as was that of the younger generation, starting with Robert Adam, and the magazine raved about Quinlan Terry's Richmond Terrace: "a remarkable piece of urban design — dignified and yet both varied and humane", and Julian Bicknell's British embassy in Moscow:

> it is outstanding. Neither flashy nor bombastic, it is a straight-forward, well-intentioned building whose neo-classicism will fit well into ... one of the older and hardly altered parts of Moscow. This is the sort of undemonstrative architecture for which England was once famous.

And all of this went hand-in-hand with applause for the Prince of Wales's attack on the architectural profession and his support for John Simpson's classically-inspired designs for London's Paternoster Square and for the London Docklands.

Country Life was the ideal vehicle for this frontal assault on Modernism. The Corbusier exhibition at the Hayward Gallery in 1987 invited its denunciation of his "bloody-mindedness which seems the most intolerable today". Instead, the post-Modernists were eulogised: Terry Farrell's work was seen as epitomising a revival of "the picturesque tradition in British architecture"; Robert Venturi's Sainsbury Wing of the National Gallery was declared "brilliant"; William Whitfield's Richmond House, Whitehall, a "remarkable building" and the work of Michael Hopkins was accorded a paean of praise. "It is remarkable", recorded Roderick Gradidge in 1988, "how quickly English architects have returned to their traditions directly the shackles of Modernism have been thrown off".

One can almost see Christopher Hussey rising from the grave to salute them. *Country Life* had been right all along, it seemed, and Modernism was demonstrated to have been an un-British activity.

For the first time since the 1960s, recently-built country houses featured

(Opposite) A neo-Greek ante-room painted in trompe l'oeil *by Alan Dodd which featured in the 'Real Architecture' exhibition in London in 1987.*

(Above) The south front of Wivenhoe New Park, Essex. Built in 1965, it derives its architectural language from the sixteenth-century Italian villa. It predicted a return to Classical tastes that matured in the 1980s.

again, such as John Outram's extraordinary New House in Sussex: "this is a natural house. Not only is it in harmony with the landscape that immediately surrounds it and with the park beyond, but once you are inside … as little as possible is put between you and the fine … countryside outside". At the same time, there was a garden renaissance with new gardens laid out in the style the magazine had promoted in its early days — that of Gertrude Jekyll and Edwin Lutyens. The return to order and formality was such that the subject of topiary was accorded a whole series of articles.

The magazine's coverage of new architecture went in tandem with attacks on building regulations which inhibited any imaginative growth of villages, allowing, for example, the building of terraces or front doors straight onto the street.

All attempts to build new villages, which were ardently supported, were stopped on appeal. This return to an interest in modest housing arose out of an acute awareness of the increasing rural poverty caused by chronic rural unemployment, low incomes and a poor housing situation exacerbated not only by the purchase of available housing stock as second homes for urbanites but also by the sale of village council houses to some existing tenants which reduced the rentable housing stock.

Time and again there were calls for further government support for the Housing Corporation, whose task it was to build houses for the less well off. The trouble was how to stop those fortunate enough to gain such a property from selling it at a handsome profit, an ironic and natural consequence of the home-ownership ideology promoted by the Conservatives.

When a survey was made in 1990 of what constituted a dream house, it concluded that it was a Georgian house with six bedrooms, large drawing room, and twenty to fifty acres of land. But by the early 1990s, the property market had collapsed.

It is too early too assess the changes made by Clive Aslet since 1993, although it is clear that a more crusading tone has begun to appear, with campaigns against rural crime and a plea for a White Paper on the countryside particularly standing out.

Only one of these topics is liable in the future to present an editor with a dilemma and that is the magazine's resolute defence of field sports which, in 1984, it defined as "the bloodstream of the nation". Of course, to abandon support for this "sport" would signal a profound disenfranchisement of the core of its traditional readership. Only time will tell if *Country Life* changes its stance on this. Perhaps the most striking innovation of all is the arrival of a strip cartoon — the hugely successful 'Tottering-By-Gently' — for a sense of humour and enjoyment is what life in country at its best is about.

(Left) Quinlan Terry's finished drawing for the facade of Merks Hall, Essex, built in 1986. Essex seems to have been a favoured site for a number of opulent Classical houses built in this decade.

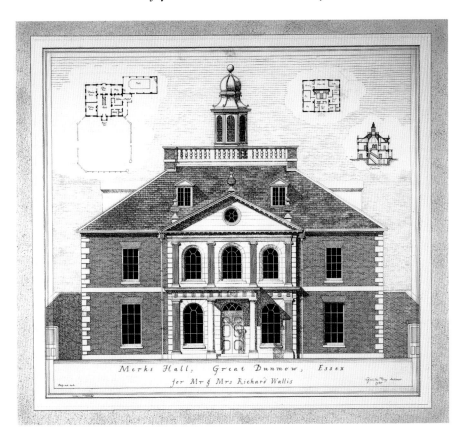

A Crowded Landscape

In June 1986, John Quicke in an article on 'The Case for lower-input farming' described the farmer's agenda for the rest of the century:

> For farmers, this is a time of uncomfortable rapid change, unprecedented in the working lives of all but the very oldest of us. Concerns that a few years ago seemed marginal — surpluses, pollution, wildlife, changing diet, landscape — are now in the centre of the stage.

The following year came an article on 'Addressing the Crisis', one precipitated by Britain's membership of the European Union and the problem of massive food surpluses which meant that up to as much as 2.47 million acres of agricultural land would have to go out of food production. *Country Life* had remained loyal to the farming cause since the 1930s and had hardly questioned the era of what it described as "ruthless farming", during which four-fifths of the country's ancient woodlands had been felled, the same amount of the chalk downlands ploughed up, vast lines of hedging ripped out and so much nitrogenous fertiliser poured onto the soil that the water supply was polluted.

The future that the European Union presented for agriculture was summed up as follows: diversification and a return to more environmentally friendly farming methods. Diversification resulted in the generation of other areas of revenue, such as the production of quality farmhouse-made foods, the use of land for forestry or recreations such as golf courses, and the adaptation of farm buildings for bed and breakfast accommodation. The altered farming methods resulted in the production of fewer food materials by more sensitive methods. The 1987 Agriculture Act designated Environmentally Sensitive Areas in which farmers had to farm in a particular way, respecting the ecological or archaeological demands of the landscape. These areas, along with the National Parks and Areas of Outstanding Natural Beauty, accounted for a large percentage of the countryside. But disquiet as to the eventual fate of what had not been so designated began to be voiced.

In June 1988 Sir Derek Barber, chairman of the Countryside Commission, wrote:

> The point to be swallowed is that, in some circumstances, the political and economic need is no longer to enable farmers to make a profit from livestock, but to subsidize, to greater or lesser degree, the keeping of animals to produce desired landscape results in the public interest.

This accorded well with *Country Life*'s increasingly green stance.

(Opposite) A magazine cover from 1987 articulating Country Life's *allegiance to the anti-road lobby which has secured support from a variety of social classes.*

THE ENGLISH ARCADIA

COUNTRY LIFE

SEPTEMBER 17, 1987 £1.20

HOW NOT TO BUILD A BYPASS

COUNTRY LIFE

SEPTEMBER 7, 1995   EVERY THURSDAY £1.90

Shy guy:
secretive
creatures of
the hedgerow

Interview with Mrs
Graham Greene

Dogs that survived
the Cold War

Cordon bleu for
the under-10s

By February 1989, an editorial headed 'Green Thoughts' urged the Chancellor to create a series of tax incentives in the interests of green causes. By the following month, it was written that: "Green politics should be part of every party's manifesto: it now seems likely that they will be." For the first time, these concerns also included animal welfare, covering experiments on animals, the treatment of livestock, the urgent need for a new moral code and the problems of genetic engineering.

But the countryside did not only need defending from the damage wrought to it by farmers. Control was urgently needed to stem its erosion by the tide of humanity pouring out from the cities and towns in search of leisure. The plight of the Quantocks in Somerset in 1986 is an oft-repeated tale: "In the last 25 years, cars and motorcycles have brought serious erosion problems. Tracks are churned up, banks are trampled bare of grass, gates are left open, heather fires inadvertently started." At the fortieth anniversary of the National Parks Act of 1949, the threat to the countryside was seen to be worse than it ever had been: the ever-increasing leisure and affluence of a car-owning democracy took its appalling toll on this over-populated island, as the countryside was transformed into a theme park for the city dweller.

But what the Thatcherite era of free enterprise, which had little sympathy for the rural voice, had unleashed was a flood of development on a scale unseen since the ribbon development of the inter-war years. From what was traditionally an overtly Conservative magazine, no words of condemnation were too strong for the Minister for the Environment, who overruled the attempts of local authorities to prevent building on the Green Belt. By 1990, Marcus Binney summed up the enormity of what had been allowed to happen in 'Time to call a halt':

Suburbia is on the march. Anyone who travels the countryside

(Left) 'The habits of the English fox are so well known that we feel we might be dispensed from stating anything here on so trite a subject' wrote the magazine in 1995.

(Opposite) The dormouse: the threatened inhabitant of the country's hedgerows and the emblem of Country Life's vigorous environmental campaigning.

(Above) The magazine's interest in rural and craft occupations continues: it is only in the countryside that such skills remain.

sees its relentless advance into the green fields around virtually every town and village. It comes in the shape of the most dismal speculative architecture ever to affront the eyes of the British home-maker. In the course of a decade the present government has steadily thrown to the winds many of the great achievements of post-war town and country planning ... in the past 10 years suburbia has begun once again to swamp large areas of the South and the Midlands ...

The government's strategy (or rather non-strategy) on the environment was viewed as a monument to procrastination by Lord McAlpine in 1994, as cars multiplied, global warming continued and more wildlife and plants became extinct. The constant call for a nationwide land-use policy and the creation of a separate Countryside Ministry has gone unheeded. The fate of the countryside continues to be decided in the metropolis by no less than four different government departments and their decisions are inevitably governed by vote-winning concerns.

To counter this (sub)urbanisation, *Country Life* called for the rediscovery of the inner city, a call that echoes, albeit in a different context, the revulsion from what the new towns had done to the countryside in the 1950s. Then the answer had been the high-rise blocks of flats of the 1960s, now unanimously reviled. Somehow a more successful inner-city formula has to be found if the countryside is not to become an ocean of suburbs serviced by shopping malls and leisure centres.

With the pressure for food production gone, which had been the lifeline of *Country Life*'s defence of traditional farming methods in earlier decades, new arguments will have to be found to justify the sanctity of the countryside, ones not based on the tenets of inherited privilege or on the eulogy of the eighteenth-century landscape. Homes for the many can no longer be denied so that the few can enjoy a privilege of space and beauty denied to the majority of the population. The polarity in the coming century will not be that of town versus country: rather, that of the inner town as well as the countryside versus the threat of suburbia.

Country Life's persistent concern with the health of village life and rural living in general was reiterated in 1987 when it celebrated its ninetieth birthday with a salutary reminder of the magazine's ideals:

> What is it about this weekly paper that has enabled it to hold the loyalty of readers and advertisers alike? Nowhere else in the western world is there a corresponding periodical that embraces so many aspects of civilisation — art, architecture, music, theatre, books — and places these good things against a rural rather than an urban background. The whole point of

Country Life is that the national culture that it reflects is set against the backdrop of the countryside. Love of our landscape is a mainspring of our existence … English civilisation differs from that of France, Germany and Italy, and the other countries of the western world, in that it is not emotionally based on cities … but it is emotionally based on the countryside …
The real danger lies in the relentless advance of urbanization.

Some things have changed since 1897. At the end of the century the magazine can no longer propound a rhetoric of national identity based on its photographic content. Britain is now a multicultural society and that fact will, as time progresses, be increasingly reflected in the composition of the establishment classes which make up *Country Life*'s future readership. Although unashamedly the voice of a privileged class and of those who aspire to join it, *Country Life* can look back with some pride on a record not devoid of achievement. The image of the countryside and the life led within it is a peaceful and reconciling concept and its adoption by the middle classes has contributed to the relatively painless social revolution this country has undergone since the beginning of the century.

Although there is a plethora of other magazines covering the ground which was once *Country Life*'s sole domain, none has yet wholly succeeded in taking over its position as the voice of rural concerns heeded by policy makers. The magazine has also significantly contributed to the preservation and wider understanding of the physical attributes of the society whose demise it mourned. No one in 1897 could have predicted that our great country houses would, by the close of this century, form the centre of a heritage cult enjoyed by all classes. *Country Life* has also pioneered the history of British architecture and art through its long line of distinguished authors, and its role in the rise of the preservation movement — in particular, its alliance with the National Trust and the Council for the Protection of Rural England — has been distinguished. Its influence in the gardening field was recognised by the prestigious award in 1995 by the Royal Horticultural Society of the Veitch medal to the magazine's long-standing gardening editor, Tony Venison.

But surely its most abiding achievement is that it holds fast to something which is increasingly rare: a consistent sense of what being British is. The magazine still stands for the civilised person in the old sense of the word, someone as much at home working in the garden as seeing an art exhibition, as fascinated by the nesting habits of birds as the restoration of a state bed, as concerned about pollution as much as who will win the Boat Race. It is in its belief in the significance of the place that a sense of rural belonging has in our national consciousness that the genius of *Country Life* resides.

(Above) A now regular rural 'type' familiar to our television screens: the anti-road protestor, here challenging the road-building lobby.

(Next page) The arcadian dream - here represented by Chatsworth, Derbyshire - which still captures the imagination of inhabitants of and visitors to this country alike.

Index

Index cont.

Picture References

Country Life Picture Library:
Barker P opp. title page, Gibside 27.10.1994. **Boursnell** C p220&221, Chatsworth 7.4.1994. **Boys M** p207, Roses at Dalmain 18.8.1988 (cover). **Drumm & Stevenson** p148, Festival of Britain site 1951. **Evans F** p23, Chateau La Rochefoucauld 1906/7; p58, Cawston Church 9.12.1905. **Gibson J** p190&191, Mavisbank 1987; p212,Wivenhoe New Park 27.7.1965. **Gill A** p31, Garsington Manor date unknown; p49, Eaton Hall 1932; p78&79, West Wycombe village date unknown; p106, Ambrose Heal room setting 1.7.1933; p107, Oliver Hill room setting 1.7.1933; p115, Penheale Manor 28.3.1925; p149, Interior for Council of Industrial Design 1951 23.5.1963. **Henson** p47, Harrow School 14.7.1934; p57, Kelmscott Manor 27.8.1921; p87, Alnwick Castle 1927; p110, High Cross Hill 11.2.1933; p121, Norfolk House 25.12.1937; p129, Kersey village 24.8.1940. **Imrie-Tait T** p213, Drawing of Merks Hall 7.7.1986. **Kitchen** p66&67, The Wyck, Hitchin 4.11.1905. **Knowles C** p219, Newbury protester 25.1.1996. **Latham** p56, Deanery Gardens kitchen 1903; p65, Elvaston Castle 21.1.1899. **Newbury** p108, High and Over 19.9.1931. **Ramsay A** p6, Plas Brondanw 15.9.1994. **Scabro** p166, High Sunderland 15.9.1960. **Sleigh** p62, Iford Manor 1922. **Starkey A** p84, Penns in the Rocks 23.3.1961; p136&137, London Skyline Country Life Annual 1963; p154&155, Bayons Manor 3.3.1960; p161, Imperial Institute 23.2.1956; p208, Danes Cottage 20.10.1983. **Upton S** p218, National Treasure Hatmaker 27.1.1994. **Ward** p114, Ednaston Manor 24.3.1923. **Westley FW** p144&145, Gribloch 12.1.1951; p109, Charters, Sunningdale 24.11.1994 & 8.12.1944; p113, Devonshire House 20.9.1919; p132&133, Blandford Forum 1947. **Anon.** p14&15, Tortworth Court 1899; p20, Baddesley Clinton 1897; p21, Mathern Palace 1910; p25, Poxwell Manor 18.4.1914; p26, Little Boarhunt 1913; p34&35, Bibuy Village 7.9.1912; p36, Trinity Foot Beagles date unknown; p38, Burnham Beeches c1897; p41, Early motorcar 14.6.1902; p44, Cockle gatherers 14.1.1905; p46, The Champion Putting 2.11.1901; p50, Miss Wilmot c1900; p63, Lutyens fountain 1908; p75, Northborough Manor 2.4.1910; p80, Chequers Court 6.10.1917; p82, Great Chalfield Manor 29.8.1914; p89, Scotney Castle 31.5.1902; p90&91, Finchinfield village 11.1.1902; p105, Claridge's 11.6.1932; p119, Dorchester House 5.5.1928; p122, Port Lymne 4.2.1933; p162, Brodsworth Hall 10.10.1963.

223

Picture References cont.

Architects Journal p203, Falmer House 28.10.1965. **Bawden WR** p169, Cotswold Hunt 26.11.1959. **Beken of Cowes** p12, Sailing & yachting 28.4.1960 (cover). **Bibbings AV** p139, Ideford Village, Devon 31.5.1946 (cover). **Bridgeman Art Library, London/Art Workers Guild** p17, portrait of Sir Edwin Lutyens as Master of the Art Workers Guild, 1933 by Meredith Frampton (1894-1984). **Bryant R/Arcaid/Designer A Dodd** p211, Neo-Greek Interior by Dodd 9.4.1987. **CLRPC** p117, Rural scene 23.5.1936. **Dalton C** p192, Great Livermere Church 7.7.1977. **Dalton S/NHPA** p216, Doormouse 7.9.1995 (cover). **Dennis Moss W** p134, Womens Land Army 9.9.1939. **Donat J** p200, Schreiber House Kitchen 5.8.1965. **Fall T** p43, Dog portraits 21.1.1911. **Farmers Weekly** p180, Crop spraying 2.7.1970. **Fawley HM** p188, Conservation corps 14.10.1971. **Fiennes M** p13, Wallpainting 21.4.1988 (cover). **Friends of Old Hall Association** p153, Gainsborough Old Hall, Lincolnshire 1.4.1954. **Greater London Record Office** p199, Hayward Gallery 1.8.1968. **Hardman J** p174, Holiday traffic 21.4.1966. **Hoppe EO** p69, Duchess of Westminster 1.1.1916. **Howard A** p153, Thornbury Castle, Gloucestershire 1.4.1954. **Hughes A** p42, Marchioness of Granby & Child 16.9.1899. **Jarvis R** p153, Doddington Hall, Lincolnshire 1.4.1954. **Jones JL** p180, Corn growing 19.12.1968. **Kersting AF** p170&171, Stratton Park 12.1.1967; p195, Ramsgate Harbour 31.7.1975. **Lampson SM** p178&179, Poodle dogs 28.12.1961. **Leggat M** p209, Rosy Carr-Ellison & Major Johnny Shaw 4.8.1988. **Luzzatto C** p176, Laura Ashley fashion 15.4.1971. **Meadows B** p187, Elmley Castle 1966. **Murray A** p173, Fashion & motorcar 14.10.1971. **National Portrait Gallery** p17, Jekyll portrait date unknown. **Nicholls HW** p77, The Officers Mess 1.5.1915. **Ogilvy DJW** p153, Winton House, East Lothian 1.4.1954. **Paton W/NHPA** p217, Fox cubs 13.7.1995. **Reid** p32&33, ploughing & plough horses 7.1.1905. **Sandersons & Sons** p177, Leafy wallpaper 9.12.1965. **Scott W** p175, Caravans 22.8.1974. **Scowen K** p165, Fishing the Thames 1963 (cover); p215, Loder Valley 17.9.1987 (cover). **Sutcliffe FM** p51, Gaffer & gammer 9.10.1909. **Tarlton J** p140, Village wheelwright 17.3.1960; p181, Ploughing paraquat 17.3.1966; p183, Scientists 12.1.1967. **Times The** p196, M23/M25 Interchange 8.4.1976. **Thompson** p95, Glyndebourne 27.5.1939; p120, Islington Square 1936. **Tomlinson D** p189, Looking at Brendon Hills 15.1.1976. **Topham J** p182, Chicken Farm 12.1.1967. **Vandyke Studio** p150, Lady Anne Coke 23.6.1950. **Warner S** p204&205, Stainforth Bridge 9.12.1989. **Wright M** p197, Motorway bridge 15.10.1970. **Wrightson H** p127, Lady Harris 30.12.1939. **Young D** p159, Portrait in New House at Leuchie 26.10.1961.

Anon. p29, Lutyens' offices for Country Life; p37, Cattistock Pack 10.2.1906; p45, George Head 4.12.1909; p47, Kennel Club 6.8.1898; p61, Cottage at Merrow 1914; p70, Women road menders 21.4.1917; p71, Women factory workers 9.12.1916; p76, Ammunition horses 23.3.1918; p83, Hampstead Garden Suburb 1914; p88, Christopher Hussey 26.3.1970; p97, Trailer caravan 28.8.1926; p98, Housing for country people 3.5.1919; p99, Drawings of cottages 1919; p100, Kitchen 29.1.1921; p101, Early cooker 12.6.1920; p116, Great West Road 5.6.1935; p124, Adolf Hitler 28.3.1936; p125, The Emergency Hut 30.9.1939; p128, White cliffs 24.8.1940; p130, Blenheim Palace 3.2.1940; p131, Lady Carnarvon 9.3.1940; p131, Child evacuees 9.4.1940; p135, Lake District farm workers 14.8.1942; p141, Thatcher's tools 27.10.1960; p143, Coronation Procession 6.6.1953; p156, Tonbridge High Street 3.9.1964; p157, Thames Street, Windsor 25.7.1963; p160, Harlow New Town flats Country Life Annual 1960; p168, M-motorway 13.8.1948; p185, Little Maplestead, Essex Country Life Annual 1964; p202, South Bank Centre 1.8.1968.

Bibliography

Aslet, Clive — *The Last Country Houses*, Yale University Press, 1982

Beevers, Donald — "Percy Macquoid, Artist, Decorator and Historian",in *Antique Collector*, 55 1984, June and July

Boyes, Georgina — *The Imagined Village. Culture, ideology and the English Folk Revival*, Manchester University Press, 1993

Cannadine, David — *The Rise and Fall of the British Aristocracy*, Yale University Press, 1990

Cornforth, John — "Lutyens and Country Life: 81 Not Out", in *Lutyens. The Work of the English Architect Sir Edwin Lutyens (1869-1944)*, Arts Council Exhibition catalogue, 1981-2

\- — *The Search for a Style, Country Life and Architecture 1897-1935*, W.W. Norton & Co., 1989

Crook, J.M. — "Christopher Hussey: A Bibliographical Tribute", in *Architectural History*, XIII, 1970

Dakers, Caroline — *The Countryside at War 1914-1918*, Constable, 1987

Darwin, Bernard — *Fifty Years of 'Country Life'*, Country Life Publications, 1947

Edwards, Ralph — "Percy Macquoid and Others", in *Apollo*, XCIX, May 1974

Elliott, Brent — *Victorian Gardens*, Batsford, 1986

\- — *The Country House Garden from the archives of Country Life 1897-1939*, Mitchell Beazley, 1995

Gill, Crispin (ed.) — *The Countryman's Britain*, David & Charles, 1986

Gill, Richard — *Happy Rural Seat. The English Country House and the Literary Imagination*, Yale University Press, 1972

Girouard, Mark — *The Victorian Country House*, Oxford University Press, 1971

\- — *Life in the English Country House*, Yale University Press, 1978

Gradidge, Roderick — *Dream Houses. The Edwardian Ideal*, Constable, 1980

Hall, Michael — *The English Country House from the archives of Country Life 1897-1939*, Mitchell Beazley, 1994

Holroyd, Michael — *Lytton Strachey, II, The Years of Achievement (1910-1932)*, Heineman, 1968

Holt, Richard — *Sport and the British. A Modern History*, Oxford University Press, 1989

Horn, Pamela — *Rural Life in England in the First World War*, Gill & Macmillan, 1984

\- — *The Changing Countryside in Victorian and Edwardian England and Wales*, Athlone Press, 1984

\- — *Ladies of the Manor. Wives and Daughters in Country House Society 1830-1918*, Alan Sutton, 1991

Mason, Tony (ed.) — *Sport in Britain. A Social History*, Cambridge University Press, 1989

Mingay, G.E. (ed.) — *The Rural Idyll*, Routledge, 1989

Mingay, G.E. — *A Social History of the English Countryside*, Routledge, 1990

Newby, Howard — *Green & Pleasant Land? Social Change in Rural England*, Hutchinson, 1979

Ottewill, David — *The Edwardian Garden*, Yale University Press, 1989

Percy, Clare and Ridley, Jane (eds.) *The Letters of Edwin Lutyens to his wife Lady Emily*, Collins, 1985

Reilly, C.H. — *Scaffolding in the Sky. A semi-architectural autobiography*, George Routledge & Sons Ltd., 1938

Richardson, Kenneth — *The British Motor Industry 1896-1939*, Macmillan, 1977

Simon, Brian and Bradley, Ian (eds.) *The Victorian Public School. Studies in the Development of an Educational System*, Gill & Macmillan, 1975

Spruling, Hilary — *Secrets of a Woman's Heart. The Later Life of Ivy Compton-Burnett 1920-64*, Hodder & Stoughton, 1984

Tankard, Judith B. — "Gardening with Country Life", in Hortus, No.30, Summer, 1994

Watkin, David — *The Rise of Architectural History*, The Architectural Press, 1980

Weaver, Lawrence T. — *Lawrence Weaver 1876-1930. An annotated bibliography*, Inch's Books, 1989

Wiener, Martin S. — *English Culture and the Decline of the Industrial Spirit*, Cambridge University Press, 1981

Williams-Ellis, Clough *Lawrence Weaver*, Geoffrey Bles, 1933

VILLAGE INDVSTRIES

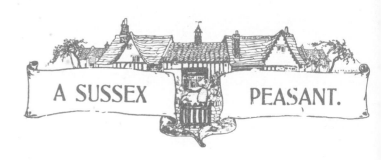

A SUSSEX PEASANT.

CORRESPONDENCE ·

THE AUTOMOBILE WORLD

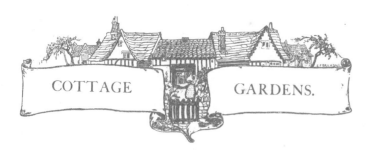

COTTAGE GARDENS.

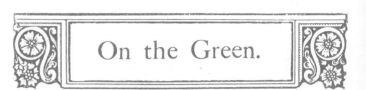

On the Green.

COVNTRY HOMES GARDENS OLD & NEW

LOCHINCH,
AND CASTLE KENNEDY GARDENS,
WIGTOWNSHIRE.
The Seat of the EARL OF STAIR.

OF GARDEN ORNAMENT

GARDENAGE AT . .
HAMPTON COURT.
By E. LAW.

FALCONRY